Say Ye  e

Say Yes to Grace

How to Burn Bright Without Burning Out

Kirk Byron Jones

**7 Grace Solutions for 7 Great Stressors
Lighten Your Heavy Load; Grace Yourself**

Soaring Spirit Press On

Soaring Spirit Press On

ISBN: 978-0-578-07337-8

PRINTED IN THE UNITED STATES OF AMERICA

Dedication

To You, the Reader.

May you be graced by your own words, ideas, and pauses as you read. Without your input, this manuscript is incomplete.

"My grace is sufficient for you...."
2 Corinthians 12: 9

GRACE: God's Reaching And Caring,
Every moment.

Say Yes to Grace

God never meant
for life
to feel
so heavy.

It is time now
to lighten
your heavy load, and
say yes to grace.

—Kirk Byron Jones

Table of Contents

INTRODUCTION

GOT GRACE?

A testimony from the popular online social network, Facebook, tells the tale of how tired and weighed down many persons, young and old, feel:

"I am tired of being tired. Tired of being tired from being tired. Tired of being tired from being tired when doing tiring things. Tired of being tired when doing tiring things while tired."

Chronic fatigue and resulting burnout has reached epidemic proporions. It is affecting persons in all walks of life, including our young, in increasing numbers. At a forum on "The Problem of Hurry in our World" held in Boston, a chaplain from a major well-known university recently stated that the most pressing problem for incoming freshman was stress. The chaplain said, "After working so hard to get accepted into this very prestigious school, they are simply tired from jumping through all the hoops."

Concern for keeping a job in precarious financial times has exacerbated the problem of stress in the workplace. Persons are being asked to do more with less, and rather than risk being replaced, workers are pushing harder and harder. For some, overload is not caused by aspiration to achieve or fear of losing a job, its cause is rather a pressing need to be all things to all people. Such people, many of them in helping professions, including ministry, health care, and social work, just find it hard to say no. They love people and they love helping even to the point of loving both more than they love themselves. For such persons, chronic self-sacrifice is a duty, if not a divine call.

Is chronic stress the price we have to pay for earnestly seeking to achieve? Must hard work constantly feel oppressive and overbearing? Does self-sacrifice have to mean self destruction? The answer to the stress of living extremely committed lives whether in school, on the job, or in service to others, lies in activating an ever-present hidden force. That force is GRACE: **God's Reaching And Caring, Every moment.**

God always has so much grace to give; all we have to do is have some. Grace never ever stops flowing, all we need to do is receive it over and over again with open hands and hearts. Grace serves to lighten our heavy living load. We don't have to wait to receive it; we can activate it whenever we choose, and we can have as much of it as we want. Grace is an inexhaustible resource that may be accessed in unlimited ways. Grace is God's smile, feeling held, a second chance, space to rest, easy does it, surprising renewal of heart. The list is magnificently endless.

Say Yes to Grace: How to Burn Bright Without Burning Out will focus on 7 Grace Solutions for 7 Great Stressors:

7 GREAT STRESSORS 7 GRACE SOLUTIONS

Fatigue	Learn to Rest
Low Self-Esteem	Live *From* Acceptance, Not *For* Acceptance
Disappointment	Loosen Strings to Needs and Expectations
Hurry	Live at a Sacred Pace
Worry	Claim Your Inner Calm
Unhappiness	Balance Aspiration with Contentment
Fear	Believe in God Beyond "God"

Say Yes to Grace is a refreshing, practical, spiritual approach to relieving stress that will teach you how to burn bright without burning out, by balancing achievement with contentment, performance with pause, and human grit with divine grace. Indeed, life itself may be defined as the sacred dance of grit and grace. And, when it comes to God's grace, there is no off switch.

Get Grace! The getting is good, resulting in optimism that doesn't burn out, and overflowing physical, mental, emotional, and spiritual energy.

CHAPTER ONE
LEARN TO REST

"Rest in the Lord."
—Psalm37:7

"It is all a rich farewell now to leaves, to color. I think of the trees and how simply they let go, let fall the riches of a season, how without grief (it seems) they can let go and go deep into their roots for renewal and sleep."
—May Sarton

"There are few things in life more dynamic than a rested soul."
—Kirk Byron Jones

Rest in a Restless World

It is Wednesday, May 7, 2008. The online headline reads: **Burma Cyclone Death Toll Past 22,000.** The story updates the latest tragedy of massive proportions. In addition to the growing number of dead, because of the cyclone, named Nargis, tens of thousands are missing and even more left homeless. Now, this in a country that was just a year ago making headlines due to brazen governmental and military oppression. My prayerful concern is for the thousands and for "the one" and his family. The one is a former student I spent many hours with in doctoral studies at Andover Newton Theological School. Just a few months after graduating, the young pastor-scholar returned home to teach in his native Burma.

How do we rest in a restless world? How do we rest in a world that time and time again breaks our hearts and makes us hang our heads in dismay and ask, "Why?" In this moment, I am not just questioning our *ability* to rest in a world that seems constantly in need of rescuing, but our *right* to. How dare we rest when there is so much that requires our sustained energized focus and attention!

How dare we *not* rest?

The Power of Pausing

On a Tuesday evening in late August, 2001, Pulitzer Prize winner trumpeter and composer, Wynton Marsalis, was playing at the Village Vanguard, one of the world's most famous jazz clubs. David Hajdu was there to see, hear, and relay this extraordinary moment:

He played a ballad, "I don't Stand a Ghost of a Chance with You," unaccompanied. Written by Victor Young, a film-score composer, for a 1930s romance, the piece can bring out the sadness in any scene, and Marsalis appeared deeply attuned to its melancholy. He performed the song in murmurs and sighs, at points nearly talking the words in notes. It was a wrenching art of creative expression. When he reached the climax, Marsalis played the final phrase, the title statement, in declarative tones, allowing each successive note to linger in the air a bit longer. "I don't stand...a ghost... of... a...chance..." The room was silent until, at the most dramatic point, someone's cell phone went off, blaring a rapid singsong melody in electronic bleeps.

People started giggling and picking up their drinks. The moment—the whole performance—unraveled. Marsalis paused for a beat, motionless, and his eyebrows arched. I scrawled on a sheet of notepaper, MAGIC, RUINED. The cell-phone offender scooted into the hall as the chatter in the room grew louder. Still frozen at the microphone, Marsalis replayed the silly cell-phone melody note for note. Then he repeated it, and began improvising variations on the tune. The audience slowly came back to him. In a few minutes he resolved the improvisation—which had changed keys once or twice and throttled down to a ballad tempo— and ended up exactly where he had left off: "with... you..." The ovation was tremendous.

With all due respect to Marsalis' magnificent gift and skill, I think the key to his memorable recovery that evening is captured in two words situated in the middle of Hajdu's recollection:

"Marsalis paused."

Each of us has a song to play in this life. Our song is distinct and unique to us. Our songs may be similar, but no two songs are exactly alike as no two persons are exactly alike. In life, we are called to play together and we are called to solo. One thing is certain, whether it be in concert with others or a solo by yourself, all music, planned and improvised, requires pauses. Where there are no rests, there is no music.

It's not easy to rest in a world that sometimes seems to despise it. The roots of such disdain can be found among influential religious reflection. A well-known historic saint of the Christian Church once prayed for strength "to fight and not to heed the wounds, to toil and not to seek for rest." A highly respected leadership guru lists "rest" in a group of obstructions to genuine growth and development. He warns, "If the idea of having to change ourselves makes us uncomfortable, we can remain as we are. We can choose rest over labor, entertainment over education, delusion over truth, and doubt over confidence." A recent newspaper article celebrated the accomplishments of a local citizen by running a story with the headline: "Who needs sleep? Not this busy mom."

In his book *Crazy Busy: Overstretched, Overbooked, and About to Snap*, Dr. Edward Hallowell draws the following conclusion:

Being too busy is a persistent and pestering problem, one that is leading tens of millions of Americans to feel as if they were living in a swarm of gnats constantly taking bites out of their lives. All the screaming and swatting in the world does not make them go away.

The legendary pastor and author, Howard Thurman, once said: "[Chronic] busyness is a substitute for the hard won core of direction and commitment." In the words of that great Motown spiritual, "What Becomes of The Broken Hearted?" it is possible to be "always moving and going nowhere."

When we go and go seeing rest as more of a *threat* than a *treat*, real menaces arise: burnout, illness, and early death.

Jesus and Rest

I began preaching at the age of 12. Consumed with a burning desire to preach and teach, I zoomed through college and seminary, and pastored my first church at the age of 22. A decade later, while working in my third church and finishing my fourth degree, my zoom turned to gloom: I burned out. One night in the middle of a sermon, I suddenly stopped preaching. I was simply too tired to go on. During my enforced respite from the pulpit, a physician's question, "What do you do to relax?" and a story from the Bible changed my life. The story is found in Mark 4:35-39:

On that day, when evening had come, he said to them, "Let us go across to the other side." And leaving the crowd behind, they took him with them in the boat, just as he was. Other boats were with him. A great windstorm arose, and the waves beat into the boat, so that the boat was already being swamped. But he was in the stern asleep on the cushion; and they woke him up and said to him, "Teacher, do you not care that we are perishing?" He woke up and rebuked the wind, and said to the sea, "Peace, be still." Then the wind ceased, and there was a dead calm.

Reading this passage during my bout with burnout

changed my life. Suddenly, I was presented with an important element of life, in general, and ministry, in particular, that I had ignored: Rest. "Jesus was in the stern asleep on the cushion." Between teaching all day long and performing a storm-stopping miracle from the bow of a boat, Jesus sleeps in the back of the boat. Jesus stopped and slept. Wow!

I soon discovered something that sparked in me a radical change of attitude and behavior towards rest: Jesus rested often; rest was a part of the natural ebb and flow of his life.

Consider the following words found in the Gospels:

"Jesus went out of the house and sat by the sea...." Matthew 13:1

"Rising up early in the morning, he went out to a solitary place...." Mark 1:35

"He went up into a desert place...." Luke 4:42

"Jesus being wearied, sat on a well...." John 4:6

There are many other texts in which Jesus is not healing, teaching, or counseling; he is resting. He is experiencing what Dr. Richard Swenson refers to as "margin," space between his load and his limits.

With so much on him, so much expected of him, so much at stake, and so little time, how was Jesus able to give himself permission to rest? And, not only to rest occasionally, but experience regular intervals of rest and relaxation? How and why was Jesus able to rest so easily and frequently?

What if Jesus believed that turning it off was as important as turning it on, that you couldn't really turn it on if you didn't really turn it off?

What if Jesus believed that there were dimensions of God, personhood, and life that could only be accessed through leisure and Sabbath?

What if Jesus believed that rest did not detract from his creative labor, but rather preserved, replenished, and ignited it?

The Circle of Rest

One of the greatest obstacles to meaningful rest is the belief that rest is somehow a waste of time, that we are more productive when we work with little rest. Chronic fatigue is a problem, fatigue is not; it is part of being human. Part of being a wise human is blessing our weariness with rest. Nothing could be farther from the truth. Look at what Jesus was able to do after his nap on the boat that night. He was able to fearlessly and creatively face chaos. How bold and innovative to speak to the storm. No one had ever tried that before.

In their book, *The Breakout Principle: How to Activate the Natural Trigger that Maximizes Creativity, Athletic Performance, Productivity, and Well Being,* Herbert Benson and William Proctor write, "*Backing off is far more effective for solving problems and generating creativity than we might have ever imagined.*" The co-authors state:

To make your escape from the downward spiral into destructive stress, you can "back off," "let go," or "release" the pressure that is bearing down on you by switch-ing on the breakout mechanism. As we have seen, that may mean soaking in a tub of water, taking a walk in the woods, listening to a Bach concerto, or retreating in solitary prayer....

Pulling the breakout trigger in any of these ways will sever past patterns of thought and emotion. At the same time, a series of helpful biochemical "explosions" will begin to bubble up inside your brain and body.

Of the various biochemical explosions Benson and Proctor highlight in their book, none is more vital than the leisure-induced release of nitric oxide, "message-carrying puffs of gas that course through the entire body and central nervous system." Among its fascinat-ing wealth of offerings, nitric oxide (the NO Molecule) enhances memory and learning by operating as a transmitter between brain synapses, increases the re-lease of dopamine and endorphins which promote a sense of well-being, and helps regulate blood flow throughout the body.

Contrary to popular belief, busyness is an enemy to creative productivity. Chronic busyness leads to weari-ness, and weariness leads to stagnating repetition. In our tiredness, we begin to repeat the same thoughts and behaviors because we don't have the energy for creativity and innovation. Rest leads to peace; peace leads to clarity; clarity leads to creativity.

As I observe the life of Jesus now, I see what I missed earlier on: the crucial link between his creative dyna-mism and his priority on respite. He seemed to always have energy to give, to share, to bless. Where did it come from? How did he stay so full all of the time? He lived in what I refer to as **"The Circle of Rest"**:

THE CIRCLE OF REST

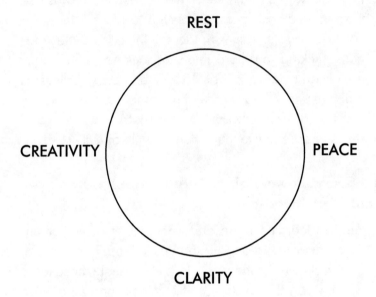

REST

CREATIVITY

PEACE

CLARITY

Rest Leads to Peace.

Peace Leads to Clarity.

Clarity Leads to Creativity.

[The Circle of Rest may be downloaded for use as a handout at www.sayyestograce.com.]

Much of our creative energy is dissipated in the constant busyness and rush of everyday life. Observing mental stillness regularly provides the openings for deeper reflection and clarity-making. How many times have you experienced an answer to a pressing concern just popping into your head while you were mindlessly involved in a leisurely task or resting? That was no accident. Your mind dislodged from intense rigid engagement was free to roam in other places, places that contained the solution you sought. This is not to say there is no place for hard thinking, but hard thinking does not hold a monopoly on creative insight. The mind in eased stillness is a potent underused source of mammoth creative energy and insight. The only way you can discover this for yourself is to dare to live the dynamic circle of rest.

The Secret Powers of Rest: Adaptability, Achievement, and Awareness

Perhaps learning more about the secret power or unsung benefits of rest will inspire us to learn to rest more. First, rest gives us the ability to better handle those times when we are blindsided by life. Things can be going so well. Our theme song is "Oh what a Beautiful Morning; Oh what a Beautiful Day," and suddenly without a moment's notice we can be hit by the turbulent unexpected: a diagnosis, an accident, a family member's confession, a friend's request, an employer's decision. If we are living with little to no rest, chances are such blows will leave us completely drained. One of the great hidden benefits of a rest habit is that it places us in a better position to withstand the surprise blows of life.

To insure that you will have the strength you need

when you least expect it, learn to rest when you're not even tired. At such times, you don't necessarily have to force yourself to sleep, just withdraw from the fray of life for a moment and hold your energy within yourself. You may do this by meditating, praying, listening to music, practicing yoga, simply being still, as well as countless other ways. In this way, you build up an energy reserve. We are so used to living with low or no energy that we don't ever imagine living with more energy than we presently need in the moment. Such reserve energy can be drawn from when crunch time arrives and living demands become unusually heavy. Reserve energy is especially valuable when we are suddenly hit with a tragic blow; e.g. the loss of a job, a dreaded diagnosis or the sudden death of a friend or loved one. Having more energy than you need should not be seen as a luxury. See it as you would a savings account: deposits intentionally stored up for the sure taxing times of life.

A second unsung benefit of rest is that it maximizes energy, turning mere energy into mighty energy. I once viewed an online video in which a highly energetic motivational speaker was encouraging teenagers to aspire to excellence. Mostly, I cheered the presentation. But, at points I jeered. The portions I objected to were those times when the speaker spoke as if rest was an enemy of achievement. At one point, he encouraged students to emulate a popular entertainer who went days without sleeping when working on projects. I objected then, and I object now. Simply put: *Rest is not an enemy of achievement; rest is a best friend to achievement.*

Moreover, rest is an even better friend to high achievement. The difference between mediocrity and optimal
achievement is often the difference between mere desire
and burning desire. Many of us wonder why it is that
we often find ourselves settling for less than we started
out expecting and desiring with our dreams.Rather than
dwindled commitment, the problem may be over-com-
mitment. Nonstop drivenness has an unintended result:
growing fatigue. In response to our dwindling energy, we
unconsciously begin to downsize our dreams to fit our
diminished exuberance. Our exuberance shrinks more
and more as we get less and less sleep and leisure. We
then pile mistaken belief on top of mistaken belief by
thinking that more power bars and drinks can enhance
our efforts. Nothing inspires when we are drained like
a good nap; there is no power drink in the world like
rest. Rest restores and revives us so that we can live our
optimal selves. Our fullest flourishing as human beings
requires that we lavishly feed growth and transformation.
The unsaluted truth is that such vital nurturing requires
not only effort, but the cessation of effort: rest.

Thirdly, rest enhances our awareness for effective
decision-making. Sometimes we are unable to make
an important decision because we are simply too tired
to do so. Fatigue is a fog that impedes clarity and
causes mental sluggishness. Chronic blurriness of mind
and weariness of body are signs that you are tired.
Deciding takes energy. Thus, if you find that there is a
decision that needs to be made, yet remains unmade,
there is a very real possibility that your problem may
not be willful procrastination, but pure fatigue. In such
a condition, the remedy is not to plow through; the
remedy is to rest. Resting gives you the opportunity to

restore your mental and spiritual energy. Once your energy is not just back, but enhanced, you are better positioned to decide with keen clarity and confidence.

We Bless the World Best when We Rest

Many have difficulty taking time to play, pause, and rest because they see it as being selfish. Whenever they do break, they are constantly haunted by feelings of guilt and the need to return to action as soon as possible. If this is your predicament, I want you to carefully consider a major shift in perception: Not taking time to rest is selfish because lack of rest insures that the world rarely sees you at your best.

Your nonstop lifestyle does not serve your interests and the interests of others as well as you may think. Living on limited rest gives the world a limited version of who you are. Being in the world constantly fatigued and chronically stressed offers the illusion of your actual presence, at best. Just because you are in attendance, it doesn't mean that you are present. We may be in attendance here or there, but when we are weary and worn, we are not wholly present. A real danger is that we can get so used to living tired, we never get a sense of who we are at our freshest and fullest. Some of us are so used to living on an "empty tank," it's hard to even imagine what living on a "full tank" feels like.

Yet, living full, flourishing, is your natural calling as an energized and empowered spiritual being. Our challenge is to reject fatigue and embrace vitality as our living norm. Moreover, living rested and well is precisely what will insure your best offering to the world no matter what your labor in life may be.

Learn to live full. Love the world enough to rest. Rest is not a sign of weakness, but a manifestation of strength. Rest is not a sign of failure, but a show of necessary faith that things can and will go on without us. Moreover, a rested you means that the world will see you at your finest. *Not resting is the selfish act. Resting is not a sign of failure or weakness; it is an act of unsung benevolence.*

We bless the world best when we rest.

Strategies for Creating a Restful Attitude and Lifestyle

(1) BEGIN YOUR DAY WITH A CALMING B.R.E.W.

Inner peace is often hard to find in our fast-paced, challenging world. Here is a delightful 4-step method to brew inner peace at the beginning of your day:

Be Still. With the assistance of candlelight and soft music, spend some of your early morning in a state of soul-quiet. One way to simply and effectively do this is to imagine something empty; e.g., an empty vase, picture frame, or house. This moment of early morning emptiness allows you to begin your day stress-free, and opens your mind to receive fresh ideas and perspectives.

Receive Divine Love. We spend so much of our energy trying to earn acceptance through meeting expectations and pleasing others. The process can be an endless tyranny because no matter how hard we try, we can't do everything and we can't please everyone, making complete acceptance seem impossible. What's the solution? Stop trying to earn your acceptance based on what you do; simply receive it based on who you are: God's Child! Stop living for acceptance. Start living from acceptance. One way to feel deep inner acceptance is to imagine yourself floating in soulfully soothing waters of unconditional love.

Embrace Yourself, Others, and Creation. The late great singer, Ray Charles, had a habit of throwing both arms around himself and rocking from side to side when he was truly happy. Take some moments each morning to embrace life. Imagine yourself hugging loved ones, new challenges, and yourself. If you can't hug you, how can you expect anyone else to?

Welcome the Day or Moment. Acknowledge each new day with a gesture of acceptance and appreciation. Affirmations are an effective welcoming strategy. Here are three of my favorite affirmations: "Today, I will play and soar in the spirit." "I will live this day at a sacred savoring pace." "This is the day I make God laugh out loud."

(2) *TAKE NON-TRAVEL VACATIONS*

Have you ever gone on vacation to a faraway place and returned feeling more fatigued than when you left? Truly invigorating vacations are more about changing what's inside of us than they are about changing what's around us. In order to feel genuine renewal, a change of setting may help but it's not necessary.

Here are four ways to have a soulfully satisfying vacation without booking a trip anywhere. How long you stay, five minutes, five days or five weeks, is up to you:

A. Let Go. Release all activities that regularly absorb energy from you, especially all work-related actions and thoughts. Genuine vacations can't happen unless you vacate your mind of thoughts that can easily and often unconsciously lure you back into work mode. A rubber band on the wrist can help you avoid thinking about work. Whenever work-thoughts surface, give yourself a little pop.

B. Lose the Schedule. Much of our daily anxiety is connected to our having to do this or be there at a certain time. True vacations take all the demand out of time.

   While on vacation, forget about having to do anything *on* time; live free and easy *in* time.

C. Delight Yourself. Engage fun, healthy, and wholesome activities for joy's sake. Submerge yourself in a spirit of play.

   Submerge yourself in a spirit of play.

D. Love the Margin. Margin is the space between our load and our limits. Such space is virtually non-existent in our "crazy busy" world. Savor the empty spaces in your vacation, the times when you are sitting, being still, and doing nothing.

(3) MIND-EASING MUSIC

"Music to sooth the savage beast" is an expression that refers to the inner peacemaking power of music. For many of us, it may have been the initial method used to calm us when our peace was broken as babies. Wouldn't it be wonderful if we all could remember the first lullaby our mothers, fathers or guardians sang to us that satisfied and soothed us? Wouldn't it be great to be able to collect some of the peacemaking songs we know and have them at the ready to help settle us down whenever we need them? Well, what are you waiting for? The latter suggestion is but an intentional action away.

Identify songs, musicians, and singers from a variety of musical genres that tend to slow you down. Take the time to create several soul-settling and inner peace-making playlists or CDs. Make sure that your peace music is easily accessible. Schedule times to sooth your savage beasts within. Just as importantly, become accustomed to taking unscheduled music breaks throughout the day. A few minutes of calming music each day adds up. The cumulative effect is a less harried and hurried soul. Here are a few of my favorite musical soul-calming CDs and artists:

The Dark Before the Dawn, Cyrus Chestnut

Heaven, Jimmy Scott

So Many Stars, Kathleen Battle

Chant I & II, The Benedictine Monks of Santo Domingo De Silos

Paganini: After a Dream, Regina Carter

First Light, Bruce Kurnow

The Intimate Ella, Ella Fitzgerald

Music of Hikari Oe I & II, Hikari Oe

New Bottle, Gil Evans

Black, Brown, & Beige, Duke Ellington

Rest for Soul Resurrection

Something surprising happened to me one morning after experiencing a moment of mental rest; I began crying for no reason at all. Why was I crying? I thought perhaps these ae leftover tears from our daughter's college graduation a few days before. Perhaps, but that didn't seem to be the right answer. I reviewed current life challenges and demands, but I could not connect my tears, which did not feel like stress or sad tears, to anything I was facing in my life at the time. Where were these mysterious tears coming from? Finally, an answer appeared that seemed like just the right answer. I had momentarily overwhelmed by calm. I was crying surprise tears of gratitude. Through my tears, I was emotionally claiming and celebrating a terribly peaceful moment of not-pulling, not-pushing, and not-striving.

There is a rest we may choose—and that may choose us—not because we are tired, but because we simply need and want to appreciate more, the music of life, between the notes. This deep sacred music has much to share with us about life, ourselves, and the ultimate meaning of life many refer to as God. This is rest that has nothing to do with alleviating physical fatigue. It is a rest of one's soul in God for peace and glad assurance. St. Augustine wrote, "Restless is our heart until it rests in God." One may not seek this rest simply because one is tired, but because one wants to be touched surely and deeply, by God.

We must learn to rest not just when we are tired or have no energy, but rest because we are convinced of the higher energizing and deeper empowerment that comes with being in communion with the depths of our souls and the soul of life itself. *We must learn to rest in peace, before we die.*

Can We Rest Too Much?

A moment ago, I referenced a speaker who was condemning rest in the name of achievement. No doubt, the speaker was condemning over-resting or laxity, which taken to extremes becomes laziness. I believe the chief indicator of resting too much is a dullness of one's creative edge. If you are being consistently creative and engaging in your interactions with others, your work, and your leisure, you can rest assured (pun intended) that you're not resting too much. If you find that you are slack and sluggish on a good sleep schedule (6-8 hours a day), naps, and a couple of 15-20 minute breaks during the day, it is possible that you are not pushing yourself enough, and needing to put more heft in your attitude and actions.

The Sweetest Pause of All

We begin this chapter with Wynton Marsalis's sweet creative pause. Though sweet, there is a pause still sweeter.

I purchased my first car when I was a senior in high school. I remember the day I picked up my Dodge Cornet, "my new used car." How can I forget it? After the transaction, I drove my car home in a driving rainstorm. It wasn't just raining cats and dogs; but to borrow a phrase from "The Wizard of Oz," it was raining "lions, tigers, and bears." I was beyond nervous; I was petrified. I remember praying, "God, please don't let me wreck my car." (When you're in danger, you don't pray long prayers.) In between driving and praying, I was doing one more thing, pausing to look in the rear view mirror. Those pauses to look, along with the praying, brought me safely home. Why was I looking in the review mirror? To catch a glimpse of my father. My dad, Frederick Jesse Jones, had driven me to pick up my car, and he followed me all the way home. Each time I paused and saw him following me, I was reassured, and knew that everything was going to be all right.

There is a pause that I call "the sweetest pause of all." It is the pause of stopping and remembering that we are the beloved of God. The sweetest pause of all is the pause of prayerfully knowing that no matter what, we are not alone.

Enlivening Affirmations

Words are wondrous! Words are wonderful! Words are magical! With words, we make meaning and create worlds. What would it mean for us to become more deliberate meaning-makers and more intentional world-conjurers? What if there are no bounds to the meanings we can make and the worlds we can form through the power of words, thoughts, and ideas? What if word power is limitless?

Affirmations are a way of using the power of words in everyday life. To that end, at the conclusion of each chapter, I will present "7 Affirmations" designed to help you cultivate and contnue a mindset of aware-ness, appreciation, and practice for the specific grace presented. Repeat these affirmations at the beginning of each day, several times a day, and before you go to sleep at night. And, don't forget to create your own word boosters. Here is your first set of affirmations:

7 Rest Affirmations

1.
Today, I swim and float in the calm refreshing waters of sustaining grace.

2.
I trust rest.

3.
There are few things in life more powerful than a rested soul.

4.
Rest is not an enemy of achievement; rest is a best friend to achievement.

5.
Rest is sweet to my soul.

6.
I bless the world best when I rest.

7.
I care to rest and rest to care.

Note to Superman and Superwoman

Life doesn't just happen

through you.

It happens

before,

around,

and

after

you.

—KBJ

Personal Reflection/Group Discussion Questions

Do you resist resting? If yes, why?

_____

_____

_____

_____

_____

What are some negative perceptions of rest?

_____

_____

_____

_____

_____

Do you believe there is a relationship between rest and creativity? Why? Why not?

_____

_____

_____

_____

_____

What are a few things you can do to make rest more of a priority?

_____

_____

_____

_____

Identify 5 benefits of rest.

_____

_____

_____

_____

Personal Journal Page

Affirmations:

_____

_____

_____

_____

_____

Questions:

_____

_____

_____

_____

_____

Reflections:

_____

_____

_____

_____

_____

CHAPTER TWO
LIVE *FROM* ACCEPTANCE, NOT *FOR* ACCEPTANCE

"We are not dipped
We are not sprinkled
We are not immersed
We are washed in the grace of God."
   —Emilie Townes

"I wish I could show you when you are lonely or in darkness, the astonishing light of your own being."
   —Hafiz

"Spirituality is less acquisition and more realization: home is within."
   —KBJ

Learning to Live Loved

The Shack, written by William Paul Young, is a journey through the valley of despair to the mountaintop of deliverance. After the abduction and murder of his beloved youngest daughter, Missy, Mack is enveloped by "the great sadness." It is sadness so deep and dark, he can hardly see which way to turn. The great sadness, however, meets its match in an even greater encounter—with God. Mack receives an invitation from God to return to the place, a shack, which contains evidence of Missy's fate. The shack, the punishing ground that symbolized Mack's worst nightmare, becomes a sacred healing ground. As he encounters manifestations of God that challenge his traditional perceptions of divinity, Mack expresses all of his pent up anger and rage, holding nothing back. And, God holds nothing back. When all is said and done, Mack's inner storm has been quieted. Jolted and perplexed by the onset of a strange but oh so soothing peace, Mack asks, "So what do I do now?" God's answers, "What you're already doing, Mack—learning to live loved."

Truth be told, Mack's calling is our calling: Our greatest common calling is to learn to live loved. We are the beloved and accepted of God. Do we dare accept our acceptance? Will you accept your acceptance?

Living *From* Acceptance not *For* Acceptance

There is a story told of the musk deer of North India. In the springtime, the roe is haunted by the odor of musk. He runs wildly over hill and ravine with his nostrils dilating and his little body throbbing with desire, sure that around the next clump of trees or bush he will find musk, the object of his quest. Then at last he falls, exhausted, with his little head resting on his tiny hoofs, only to discover that the odor of musk is in his own hide.

So often, the musk deer's fate is our own. We push and pull so hard and so often to be acknowledged and affirmed. This inner drive to be accepted can get out of hand when the acceptance is not easily won, and we end up overreaching for it in our relationships and on our jobs. Additionally, many of us know that the acceptance feeling tends to wear off pretty quickly when it is over-linked to achievement and accomplishment. Almost immediately we begin to desire a higher degree of acceptance associated with a higher level of achievement. The end result is the maddening tyranny of never feeling fully satisfied.

Thankfully, there is a clear way out of such a predicament. *That way is living from acceptance, not for acceptance.* Grace is the difference between living from acceptance and for acceptance. Living from acceptance is living with the firm belief that you are eternally embraced in the most exquisite love of all, God's love. Such glorious internal acceptance is not based on what you do, but who you are.

Most importantly, God's love is all-encompassing and all-fulfilling. We are the created love-children of God, conceived and created by love, for love. Living with the glad awareness and assurance of God's love within, eliminates the need to overreach for acceptance elsewhere, ever again.

Three Fabulous Fruit of Living *From* Acceptance

Living already filled with that which we need most: un-conditional, never-ending acceptance unleashes a vast assortment of sweet savory fruit for living, including the fabulous fruit of a *relaxed spirit, a kind heart, and a creative fire.*

So much of our existence is weighted down by our not accepting ourselves. To not accept who we are is to place a great burden on our backs. It is to be con-stantly weighed down by the notion that we are not good enough as we are, and any worth that we have any right to must be earned and re-earned by constant struggle and toil. Living in non-self-acceptance carries the additional burdensome baggage of suspecting that others don't accept us. This often triggers drivenness, feeling we have to do and overdo to make it in life, to get people to like us, and to maintain a sense of our responsibly pulling our rightful weight in the world.

The tyranny of it all transforms life into a constant push and pull existence, which causes us to feel chronically tired and worn. We live under continual duress, uneasy, unsure and unsteady in our inner and outer worlds. We do not know peace. Rarely are we content: completely satisfied with our choices, decisions, and actions. Many of us know the words to the song "It is Well with My Soul," but how often is it really well?

There is a way to heal our over-strained hearts and relax our restless souls. David Steindl-Rast writes in his wonderful book, *Gratefulness: The Heart of Prayer,* "To accept God's acceptance of us makes self-acceptance possible." Having and cultivating an abiding sense of inner validation via sacred gift provides for peace dislodged from productivity, others' opinions of us, and over-fixation on obligation. The end result, at first, takes our breath away. It is an easing of our heavy load, the diminishing of the usual unyielding pressure of life, and the onset of a more relaxed inner spirit. When our spirits are relaxed, we don't begrudge life, we behold it; we cherish it. This is living loved, the brightest, lightest thing you'll ever imagine and discover.

Living from acceptance yields another truly astounding benefit: affirmation of others. It brings to a dramatic conclusion our needing to compete with others for acceptance. So much of our feeling good about ourselves hinges on competing against, or worse, condemning others. We all know persons who seem to know no other way of looking good apart from making others look bad. Lavish inner acceptance has no need to compete or judge. Its identity shines on its own and has no need to diminish or denigrate others. So magnificently secure from within, we are less likely to see others and others' gifts as threats to ourselves and what we have to offer. There are no more struggles against others for attainment and notoriety. We are the notoriously blessed from within, free to be and free to love, without fear.

Self-acceptance leads to other-acceptance. Both lead to a tremendous savings in energy, and I am not talking about your electric bill. No longer needing to expend energy on our insecurity and selfishness, we are filled with excess energy for more creative pursuits in the world. We spend so much energy trying to be accepted, noticed, and loved, and then trying to protect whatever status we think we have earned in the world. What marvelous things are possible when energy no longer needs to be concentrated on earning and protecting what we come to know as the *Grand Gift that can never be taken away*—God's love! Not needing to seek what we already have and clutch what cannot be stolen, there is suddenly within each of us a well of surplus power for previously unimaginable inspired creative pursuits in the world. There are few things more powerful in the cosmos than a soul aflame with the love of God.

The Color of God's Eyes

As appealing and inviting as it may sound, learning to live loved and accepting our acceptance can be a mighty challenge. From time to time, I write brief spiritual comments on Twitter and Facebook, the two major online social network sites. In the summer of 2010, I posted the following:

"Know who you are in God's eyes; then, dare to look at yourself through the eyes of God."

Most of the responses affirmed the sentiment, some giving it the little Facebook thumbs-up "like it" sign. But, two responses caused me pause and reflection. Each, in their own way, spoke deeply and honestly about difficulty feeling loved, even by God. One person wrote,

"Some folks would be blinded, Rev. Kirk. As for myself, I would have to close my eyes quick."

Another said:

"I try doing this but I think I am telling God what to see... How do you get his vision????"

Feeling God's love, for some, is easier said than done. I thought about what might hinder our reception of the mightiest love in the cosmos—indeed the love from which the cosmos emanates and continues to expand. I suspected some leading candidates might be guilt, shame, and fear. These feelings can weigh us down so much that it feels next to impossible for anything to raise us up. Diminishing feelings, feelings that shrink us, may get between us and God's love. But, feelings about ourselves aren't the only sentiments that may try to stand between us and God's love, our perceptions about God may as well.

Later in this book, I'll discuss in greater detail the practical significance of our perceptions of God. Suffice it for me to say here that if we view God mostly as judge and jury, then it is difficult to see God's grace first and foremost. In our sight, God's holy eyes burn like fire on our perceived ungodliness.

God's sight is different. Seeing ourselves through God's eyes blesses us immeasurably, if we can believe that God's eyes are colored grace.

To my beloved honest Facebook confessors, thank you for sharing your heartfelt sentiments. I do not know what it was exactly that motivated your response. But to you, and for all of us: There is a reality beyond our most damning views of ourselves and our most demanding perceptions of God. This Reality is the God of Wild and Wonderful Grace. Such grace always sees through it all to the truest truth of all: no matter what, *we are and always will be the beloved of God. God loves us and there is nothing we can ever say or do to make God stop loving us. Should we say "no" to God; God will never say "no" to us.*

Listen to Your Mental Chatter

If we are to accept our acceptance and live from it, it will involve monitoring our mental chatter. People who talk a great deal are sometimes referred to as chatter boxes. While we all may not be chatter boxes; each of us has a chatter box: our minds. Before we get up in the morning, our minds are at work presenting us with this or that idea and notion. When the ideas are predominately negative, the end result is, as the popular expression goes, our "getting up on the wrong side of the bed." Sometimes the early chatter is so dismal we have no alternative: there is no right side of the bed.

Pay attention to your morning mental chatter, and your chatter throughout the day. Observe your thoughts, especially those sentiments that appear easily in your mind when you are not trying to think about anything at all. These are your regulating default thoughts, thoughts that you are so used to thinking that you don't even think about them. What does mental chatter have to do with learning to live loved? Mental chatter rooted in fear, shame, regret, and guilt can render us unreceptive of and nonresponsive to God's love. Whether the soul-diminishing rhetoric is directed at ourselves or others, the impact is the same: continual construction of barriers that prevent us from fully receiving and flourishing in God's love. I believe that hell is the unending denial and refusal of God's love. Thank God, eternity is God's relentless love.

Replace Loveless Chatter with Love-Filled Chatter

While away on a speaking engagement, I had an amazing thing happen to me one morning. As I started to arouse from sleep, I heard an inner voice say, "Good morning, child of God." Though, not an audible voice, the pronouncement startled me with its clarity and directness. I remained in bed thinking about what I'd just heard. What did it mean? Where did it come from? How could it meet me so firmly and finely in my first waking moments? I kept replaying the strange powerful greeting in my mind, each time owning a little bit more of the potent affirming message it carried. Moments later, while preparing to shave, I stared at the face in the mirror longer than usual. Soon, I heard the greeting again, "Good morning, child of God." This time the voice was audible; the voice was my own.

"Good morning, child of God" is more often than not my first thought of the day. I embrace it as a sacred reminder of who I am apart from roles, masks, expectations, obligations, and achievements. The phrase allows me to bask in the glow of divine affirmation at the start of the day. The effect is an attitude of humble confidence, and the holy gift of *living from acceptance, not for acceptance*. People often say that beauty is in the eye of the beholder. The point of greatest liberation for the beholder is realizing that she is the beauty.

We may choose any time we wish to substitute the chatter of diminishment with the chatter of empowerment. First thing in the morning is a good time to do this. Listen to love-filled chatter early, before you rise or soon after. It allows you to hear your affirming words on a clear channel. At the beginning of the day, you have yet to be bombarded with all the messages your mind is soon to get from everywhere, including family, job, and the world at large. The early morning self-love talk does not have to fight to be heard over all the other voices. Another reason for early love-filled chatter is that it serves as a *positive mental set-point* for the rest of the day. See it as setting your mental thermostat. Setting a thermostat in a home or building is a method for assuring a sustained comfortable environmental condition. Setting our hearts and minds on love first thing in the morning has the prospect of drawing all we think and do to that magnetic set-point throughout the day.

Believe that God Loves You Madly

Legendary composer, pianist, and bandleader, Edward Kennedy "Duke" Ellington, had a signature expression for closing each concert. Speaking for himself and his renowned band of musical masters, Ellington would smile and say to his audience, "Remember, we do love you madly." It was his standard closing line, and he learned to say it in many different languages. With all due respect to one of this and any other world's great creative geniuses, I think Duke is appropriating and repeating a sentiment previously expressed—by God.

I believe Duke Ellington was able to express mad love so freely because he grew up believing himself to be madly loved by God. The most significant human man-ifestation of such love was his mother, Daisy Kennedy

Ellington. Ellington said he grew up hearing repeatedly from her, "Edward, you are blessed. You don't have anything to worry about. Edward you are blessed." We are all the beloved and blessed of God. Can we live in the warm sunlight of such grand acceptance?

Can you believe the following? You are no less loved by God than anyone else; you are no less God's child than anyone else. God's love is the most pervasive and potent reality in the entire universe. Since the universe includes you and me, this means that God's love is lavishly spread inside each of us. With this in mind, know that you are loved, lovely, and lovable! God is love; you are God's; you are loved. I believe this is what Jesus meant when he said to persons time and time again, "The Kingdom of God is within you."

Do you dare believe any of this? Do you dare not to believe any of this?

Remember Love

Since we are in love and love is in us, the spiritual journey may be interpreted as a pilgrimage toward *awareness* and *acceptance* of God's love. We may also speak of this process or transformation as *remembering* that we are loved. With this in mind, I offer the following "remembrance strategies" for your consideration:

1. Notice God's Love. God shows signs of magnificent affection through persons, nature, and situations all the time. Slow down, pay attention, and savor life more.

2. Visualize Receiving God's Love. Be still and relax

your mind. Once you feel relaxed enough, envision yourself being loved by God in meaningful ways. Here are some possibilities: (a) See yourself being refreshed beneath the majestic waterfall of God's love. (b) Take an imaginative swim in the invigorating ocean of God's love. (c) Relax all the tension in your body as you let God hug and hold you. (For a touching example of receiving and resting in love, see John 12:1-3.)

3. Affirm God's Love. Words and beliefs are significant building blocks we use to help construct our living reality every day. Affirmations are worded beliefs that we can either say aloud or utter silently to remind us of God's dynamic love. Here are three of my favorite affirmations that always sooth my soul with a refreshing sense of God's love:

"Good morning, child of God."

"I relax free and easy in God's soft grace."

"I feel the force of God's Spirit moving mightily within me."

May you remember and keep remembering that you are the beloved of God, to the point that this best truth of all becomes not just second nature to you, but first and final nature.

Trust that Love Changes the Rules and the Game

I remember hearing a story about a youngster with Down syndrome who played little league baseball. It had been a tough season in which he failed to even make contact with the ball when he was up at bat. He struck out each time. Towards the end of the season, his drought ended. He hit a ball that dribbled down the first base line. He was easily thrown out, but the moment was memorable for more reasons than one. The youngster not only made contact with the ball for the first time all season, but after being thrown out at first, he kept on running toward second base, and then on to third. Along the way, the crowd, home and visitors alike, got caught up in the player's elation. Everyone cheered loudly when he triumphantly crossed home plate.

Love not only changes the rules; love changes the whole game. Know yourself to be loved fully from within, and life will never again be the same.

I believe that the great heart-truth of the Gospel is this: Spirituality is not about being God or playing God; it's about being loved by God. Will you let God love you?"

Question at 3 AM

Will you

claim the

elegant expanse

of your

Holy Spirit?

—KBJ

What is it to Feel Loved?

A place of

not-strain and not-struggle

not-pushing and not-prying

not trying to be noticed and accepted.

Lighted and lifted

from the outside in

and from the inside out.

Freed from all

obligatory response

and all requisite demands

because pure love rests easy in its own fulfillment.

—KBJ

Morning Greeting

This morning,

while praying,

I passed by

several angels,

each one

greeting me,

in the same way,

"Good morning,

child of God."

—KBJ

Wow; Wow!

We look outside
at a beautiful day
and say, "Wow!"
The angels look inside
at our beautiful souls
and say, "Wow!"

—KBJ

7 Acceptance Affirmations

1.
I leave my heart open for God's Love.

2.
Good Morning, Child of God!

3.
God's love fills me with a natural sense of well-being.

4.
I play and soar in the Spirit.

5.
I am a whirling twirling dancing spirit!

6.
I stand tall and walk strong in God's love.

7.
I am learning to live loved.

Personal Reflection/Group Discussion Questions

How importance is self-acceptance?

_____

_____

_____

_____

_____

What are some obstacles to self-acceptance?

_____

_____

_____

_____

_____

What does knowing that you are loved by God do for you?

_____

_____

_____

_____

_____

How do you experience God's love?

_____

_____

_____

_____

_____

How might you more effectively communicate God's love to others?

_____

_____

_____

_____

Personal Journal Page

Affirmations:

_____

_____

_____

_____

_____

Questions:

_____

_____

_____

_____

_____

Reflections:

_____

_____

_____

_____

_____

CHAPTER THREE
LOOSEN ATTACHMENT TO NEEDS AND EXPECTATIONS

"I shall not want."
    —Psalm 23:1

"I walk lighter so much lighter, since I laid my burden down."
    —Gospel Song Lyrics

"Willing others to change is a big factor in burnout."
    —Margaret Marcuson

"Of all the people in the world, you can change only one."
    —KBJ

Confronting Need-Overload

How much of the stress in your life is related to what you believe to be an unmet need, longing, or expectation? Perhaps you wanted a person to do something, and it still isn't done. Maybe you've had a dream for years that has yet to come true. Or, perhaps, your need is to be different in some way, and you are growing more and more impatient, because the change, be it in weight or appearance, or something else, is still unmet.

Enough of my suggesting needs you may have. Let me ask you to stop reading the manuscript at this point and make a list of things that you believe you need to have a better life. As you make your list, you may want to use one or more of the following lines to trigger your thought-flow:

I wish I had.....

My life would be better....

I really need....to happen for me.

Once you've finished with your needs list, review it with this question in mind: How much stress am I feeling about this unmet need?

One or two unmet needs can cause much stress. Certainly the cumulative total of all the unmet needs can weigh us down consciously and unconsciously.

Allow me to suggest three methods for not letting our needs get the best of us. First, we may decide that what we thought we needed, we don't need any more. We can de-need ourselves. You may do this right now.

Review your list of needs. Which of them may be cancelled out as something you no longer deeply desire or need?

A second solution for dealing with need-overload is loosening our attachment to our needs. You don't have to rid yourself of such needs entirely, but you may rid yourself of over-connecting them to your peace and wellness. In other words, you hold them more lightly and loosely in your mind and heart. You would love for them to be met, but if they remain unmet, you will not be the lesser for it. Your peace is not dependent on the fulfillment of your need.

The third solution may be the most difficult, yet most effective of all. It is choosing to live as need-free as you possibly can.

Challenging the Need to Need

We weigh ourselves down with too much that weighs us down, and one of the weightiest things of all is our need to need. What if it were possible to choose not to need as much as we choose to need? *It is possible.* It is possible to learn to live more lighthearted and free, not overly attached to anything, anyone, or any need. After physical nourishment, basic material sustenance, healthy relationships, and viable creative expression, what more do you really *need* to live a fulfilled life? Freed from excessive needs, we can live graced, more lighthearted and free.

Contentment is a matter we'll take up more fully later in the book. But, allow me to address it a bit now. Contentment is a place of no-need, and not needing in order to be fulfilled. It is a place and space of feeling fully filled. Contentment is choosing to know that you don't "need" to be blessed more than you have already been blessed. It is knowing that, in the words of the biblical poet-king, David, "my cup is running over."

Needing to need takes energy from our being grateful for all we have now. And the fact of the matter is most of us living in the United States have so much more than our sisters and brothers in many economically impoverished areas of the world. A startling sentence in the important book, *Affluenza: The All-Consuming Epidemic*, places the matter in humbling perspective: *"Since 1950, we Americans have used up more resources than everyone who ever lived on earth before."* I sometimes feel ashamed that I who have so much to be thankful for can all too easily become disenchanted when just one of my wants is not denied, but merely delayed. It is possible to become blinded by "much" to the point of not seeing how much we have to be grateful for. Ingratitude is fueled by focusing on needs as opposed to blessings. It is amazing how focusing more on our blessings lessens our needs, and diminishes our need to need. It is possible to be so busy being thankful for what you already have that you don't have time to "need" anything else.

Practicing Continual Radical Gratefulness

David, the great biblical poet-king, was not beyond asking God for anything. In Psalm 7:1, he asks God for protection and deliverance. In Psalm 26:1 and 12, his request is for vindication and redemption. In

Psalm 28:9, David moves beyond asking for himself to seeking salvation for the nation. Perhaps the most admirable, albeit anguished, request of all is related in Psalm 51:10-12. In the wake of an act in which David was, to borrow a phrase I once heard preaching titan Gardner Taylor use, "disloyal to that which was royal inside of him," he pleads for God to, "Create in me a clean heart."

Yet, David's relationship with God went beyond him always asking God for things. Notably, his momentous 23rd Psalm is devoid of any request of Divinity. Indeed, there is a clue in the very first verse that there will be no requests here. David writes, "I shall not want."

In place of constantly needing, we may *substitute continual radical gratefulness*. To live continually grateful is to regularly and intentionally feed our minds with thoughts of thankfulness. It is living with a keener vision of the gifts in life, and the gift of life. To live this way is not to look away from the trials of life, but to see that even in life's trials, there is something to be thankful for. To practice continual radical gratefulness is to learn to be thankful deliberately, no matter what.

A posture of continual radical gratefulness need not eliminate needing entirely. There is a good deal of positive life energy associated with feeling and meeting needs that enhances us as human beings, and help bring justice to our world. Continual radical gratefulness simply roots our needing in the soil of deep gratitude. We learn to need from a place of fulfillment. We learn to need *from* fulfillment, not *for* fulfillment. The difference between needing *from* fulfillment and not *for* fulfillment is the difference between peace and anxiety. There is a big difference between needing from an empty cup, and needing from a cup that is always running over.

From a spiritual perspective, there is more to this matter. Continual radical gratefulness repositions our relationship with God. It is very easy to have a needs-only relationship with God. In this kind of spiritual communion, we are constantly asking God to do something for us. While it is valuable to view God as our ultimate source, there is much to be said for desiring God's *presence* more than God's *presents*. One of the most powerful benefits of enjoying God for God is the dissolving of needs. It is in experiencing God for God's presence more than God's presents that something wildly wonderful happens: *We begin to realize we already have in lavish portions all we truly need.*

Loosen Your Grip on Expectations

I was astonished and amused by what the salesperson told me. He recounted the time a customer decided not to purchase an item because she thought the price was too high. Instead, she drove six miles to another store to make her purchase. While there, she was ticketed for a parking violation to the tune of $40. Believe it or not, the customer returned to the first store in a rage, blaming the salesman for causing her misfortune. She adamantly declared, "If you hadn't charged me more for the product in the first place, I would not have had to drive to the other store."

How wildly unreasonable, and widely practiced! The truth is we slap ourselves and each other with unrealistic expectations all the time. Making unreasonable demands and trying to live up to the same is the source of tremendous living stress. What's the solution? One potent answer is checking our tendency to over-expect from others and ourselves. To take it one step further, an unsung emotional sweet spot is learning to live lightly and loosely with *all* expectations. It's not a matter of not having expectations whatsoever, but not allowing expectations to determine our happiness and peace in the world.

The question may be raised, "Don't we render persons a disservice when we expect less or nothing of them?" Challenging others to reach higher can be an act of love. But, however noble an expectation, to overly-fixate on it is to overly narrow life. There is always so much beyond our expectations.

Loosening our attachment to expectations lightens our living load immensely. Think of the load lifted as we learn to actively engage everything without over-expecting anything. Take disappointments in relationships for instance. The real sting of behavior upsetting to us lay not in the deed, but in the unmet expectation. It's not just that "Bill" or "Barbara" did what they did, but that they did not do what we expected them to do. They dared to act out of the realm of our expectation. More than the deed itself, it is the unmet expectation that sorely wounds. As we resist clinging to expectations, unrealistic and otherwise, something truly amazing happens: outcomes lose their power to upset us so. *Loosen your grip on expectations, and outcomes loosen their grip on you.*

Well, I've used many words to say what Jesus says in five, "Do not worry about tomorrow."

Pure Love Sets Us All Free

The people you love the most can be the greatest danger to you.

Do not stop loving; just be aware of this perhaps unsettling reality in ways that you have not allowed yourself to be aware of before. Sometimes "the best" someone wants for you is what serves them best. When this happens, they are, in fact, placing a deadly demand on you, one that satisfies them while diminishing you. Unchecked, you may become a co-conspirator in your own continued diminishment by habitually placing the selfish desires of others above your own soulful ones, resulting in the slow but sure decay of your soul.

It is easy to bow to selfish desires when they are expressed by those you feel closest to. But, do this often enough and you will end up choking your inner self to death. You become the person others want you to be, and not the person you want to be. The life you end up living is the role others concoct for you and not the one you ultimately create with your inner voice and God.

In your deepening awareness of this possibility, make sure that you model, as best you can, a purer love: *Love that loves with no strings attached.* As often as you can, bestow this love onto others. As others do likewise, such purer love becomes a living model for everyone, an enchanting field of free expression for all, where authentic selfhood flourishes.

The grand prize of pure love is becoming our true selves.

Peace: The Prize of Pre-emptive Detachment

How often have you let the same behavior, often by the same person, upset you over and over again? Think about it for a moment. Who's most to blame for this unrest in your life? *You are.* This person has proven to you time and time again that they tend to behave in this way. Why do you let them repeatedly agitate you with the same matter? The real truth is that they are not upsetting you; you are upsetting yourself by choosing to react the same way in response to someone's known predictable behavior. Somehow, for whatever reason, you have become attached to a habitual response to someone's habitual behavior. Here's an affirmation that will help you break this debilitating and stressful, and cultivate empowering peace in your life:

"I can't change the actions of others, but I can manage my own responses to their actions."

In light of this liberating affirmation, try this advanced response strategy. Use the past to change your future. Since you already know in advance that a person is likely to behave in a certain way (perhaps in spite of repeated requests from you to act otherwise), change your response in advance. Decide ahead of time that no matter what, you will not be upset by a known likely behavior. Claim your peace in advance. See yourself at peace before the assault on your peace begins, while it is occurring, and after it has ended. Imagine this in your mind several times. Now, if the behavior actually occurs in the future (and it may not, people don't

always act in ways we believe they will) you are prepared. Simply live your prepared-in-advance peaceful
response.

Why not?

The Healing of Letting Go

There is great healing wellness and wholeness in letting go. I am not speaking of just letting go of obvious
health strainers like guilt, shame, stress, and worry, but
letting go of expectations, scripts, roles, and masks.
We all live with demands we make of ourselves and
others that have us living out plans we perceive to be in
our best interest, and the best interests of those we care
about. These plans lead us to do certain things and
wear different garb in the process. To a large extent,
life is plan-making and role-playing. At times, we go
through the process without a hitch. It is what we do.
But, there are other times, when what we do, the demands and obligations of it all, can feel so heavy and
over-bearing. At such times, letting go of and dropping
as much as we responsibly can, can be the healthiest
thing in the world for us to do.

In order to effectively let go, we must face our resistance to doing so. For some, letting go feels too much
like negligence. This view is backed by the belief that
life is *supposed* to be heavy. Such a belief suggests that
to be a truly successful person one needs to be doing a
lot of things most of the time. When the load feels light,
it means we are not doing our share. For those who
live with this mental tape playing in their minds, it may
take some doing, but you will have to consider playing some new tapes that balance the grit of life with

the grace of life. What if life is less about doing it all, and more about enjoying the ease, easy, and ecstasy of it all. It is not that we need to totally abandon a "grit perspective." Situations will call for us to push, and push hard, but to live stuck in push-hard gear is to risk missing out on the *grace-gear* of living. Interestingly enough, Jesus presents the arduous task of following him, not in grit terms but in grace terms: *Come to me, all you that are carrying heavy burdens, and I will give you rest. Take my yoke upon you, and learn from me; for I am gentle and humble in heart, and you will find rest for your souls.* Matthew 11:28-29

In addition to a mental tape that believes life should be hard and burdensome, another formidable obstruction to letting go is feeling that when we let go we will have nothing else to hold on to. We resist relational and work transitions that we know we need, for fear that if we do let go we will be lost. We determine, perhaps more unconsciously than consciously, "Better to languish in familiar discomfort than be lost in an unknown destination." Yet, such letting go of the familiar turned frustrating is necessary for our growth and transformation. In a prayerful pronouncement that is as beautiful as it is true, Rabindranath Tagore reminds us that we should never be duped into believing that what we have is all we have:

But I find that Your will knows no end in me, and when old words die out on the tongue, new melodies break forth from the heart; and where the old tracks are lost, new country is revealed with its wonders.

Finally, we may resist letting go because we equate loving

with holding and embracing. Yet, love does not just gather unto itself; love releases. There are times when the most loving thing to do is to let go. Perhaps it is most challenging of all to love in this way, and one of the most painful lessons of all is learning to love through letting go.

I believe love releasing is a sign of love in its purest expression. Love, free, fine, and full has no needs; it is its own fulfillment. Refusing to release in the name of love is one of the surest indicators that love is waning. Pure love does not need to or seek to hold on to survive. Its livelihood is in its being free from anything or anyone for its flourishing. Its soaring is uninhibited by expectations and obligations. *Moreover, though love will savor love if returned, pure love does not need to be loved in return. Pure love is amazingly, mysteriously, and ever so majestically unconditional.*

Have a Grace Massage

We cannot give what we do not have. It is impossible to live ready, willing, and able to offer grace if we don't have it to offer. Graced people grace people. Before you can give some grace, you have to get some grace. One of the ways to feel grace all over is to get a grace massage. Your masssage can last five minutes or an hour. You decide. Here's how it's done:

1. Find a comfortable setting, and place your body in a relaxed position, either seated or lying down.

2. Take a moment to quiet your mind.

3. Focus your attention on your toes and repeat, "I

feel God's grace warming my toes." Take a moment to feel God's loving and soothing touch.

Work your way up your body, focusing and repeating the grace blessing for the portion of your body you are concentrating on. Remember to feel the blessing of God's touch each time. You can be as specific as you'd like, but be sure to include your legs, midsection, back, chest, arms, neck, and head.

4. When you are done, take a moment to savor your freshly graced body and being.

Ritual of Release

A strategy I use for preaching preparation may be appropriated for learning to grace others with the freedom to live on their terms and not ours. After I've prepared the sermon and before I actually preach it, I take a moment to let the sermon go. My favorite ritual for this is visualizing the sermon as a bird flying away from my hands. The intention is to free myself from being overly attached to preconceived sermon presentation and outcomes. I responsibly have an idea of what I'd like the sermon to accomplish, but to be too fixated on that would be to limit the sermon to doing what I want it to do. The best preaching is honed as much in the moment by the setting, congregation, and God's spirit, as it is by prior preparation. My ritual of release is a strategic reminder of that fact. With all due respect to my creative contribuitons, the sermon must be free to fly and forge, on its own terms and in its own way.

Similarly, though we, especially as parents, responsibly

contribute to the growth and development of others, we must resist demanding that persons end up being formed in our preferred images. Our investment must be demand-free in terms of final outcome. People, especially our children, must be free to be who they are and are becoming on their own terms, not ours. When we over-obligate our children to live according to our plans, we prevent them from freely and fiercely living their own uniqueness in accordance with God's designs.

The fringe benefits of letting go are enormous. What we let in by letting go are possibilities that transcend our best desires: *a soul-ease that comes with freeing ourselves from the excess weight of expectation-fixation, and the anticipatory delight of wondering just how it is that what we have freed will be framed, formed and fashioned by a fiery-free God of incomparable creative genius.*

HERE ARE SOME SAMPLE RELEASE RITUALS:

1. Imagine your desired preference for someone. See that preference on a scroll. Feel your attachment to your preference, owning each one of them. When you are done naming and owning every feeling you have for the desired preference, toss the scroll into an imaginary flame.

2. Imagine your desired preference for someone or some outcome. Think about why it is that you want what you want so much. When you are done, see yourself burying your preference in an imaginary grave.

3. Imagine your desired preference as a bird. Consider the beauty of the bird and your relationship to it. When you are ready, lift your hands and bid the bird farewell.

Prayer: Brewing a Fresh Pot of Peace

Learning to live unattached from needs and expectations will be a process. One of the best strategies for assisting us in this process is prayer. *Prayer is like brewing a fresh pot of peace.* To understand this better, consider two unsung dynamic dimensions of prayer that help us to replace debilitating anxiety, as a result of attachment fixation and otherwise, with a delicious sense of all-is-wellness.

First, prayer is letting go. One of the great prayer songs I grew up with is entitled, "Take Your Burdens to the Lord and Leave Them There." Life can be so heavy because of the loads circumstances place on us, the loads others place on us, and the loads we place on ourselves. Prayer is a time of load releasing. How much you release is entirely upon you. A great grace available to us all is that we can let go of all. That's right! For a splendid moment in time, prayer offers us a way to be completely free of *all* that presses us down and holds us back.

Second, more than it is speaking, prayer is listening. The talking aspect of prayer is undeniable. In fact, for most of us, our first experience with prayer is being taught to "say our prayers." In most of the great religious traditions of the world, however, it is the *non-saying* dimension of prayer that is seen as the most enhancing and enthralling experience of prayer. The reason is this: *As we restrict speech and thought in prayer, we open ourselves up more to God on God's terms, and not ours.* In this *purer* form of prayer, our depths are showered with the depths of God. *Pure prayer,* prayer as silence and stillness, invokes *Pure God,* God who is always beyond our finest words and highest thoughts. Letting ourselves down into the depths of God, no holds barred, is one of the most peaceful experiences we can have in this life. For some it may sound frightening, but have you ever thought about how similar the words *scared* and *sacred* are? They possess the exact same letters, just arranged differently. You don't have to be a monk or another type of "professional holy person" to experience this deeper realm of prayer. All you have to do is desire, and not resist. And get this: *you can brew a fresh pot of peace through prayer anyplace and anytime.*

7 Loosened Strings to Needs and Expectations Affirmations:

1.

"I do not expect anyone to live according to my script."

2.

"I free my loved ones to soar as God gives them flight."

3.

"I practice continual radical gratefulness."

4.

"I practice mighty gratitude, potent in constancy and tenacity."

5.

"Graced people grace people."

6.

"I love others with no strings attached."

7.

"I serve grace knowing that grace serves me."

Personal Reflection/Group Discussion Questions

_____

_____

_____

_____

What specific needs and expectations do you need to loosen?

_____

_____

_____

_____

What keeps us from loosening and letting go of things that diminish us?

_____

_____

_____

_____

How do we harm ourselves and others through over-fixating on needs and expectations?

_____

_____

_____

_____

Identify five benefits of loosening our attachments to needs and expectations.

_____

_____

_____

_____

How do we balance limiting expectations with encouraging ourselves and others to achieve and succeed?

_____

_____

_____

_____

Personal Journal Page

Affirmations:

_____

_____

_____

_____

_____

Questions:

_____

_____

_____

_____

_____

Reflections:

_____

_____

_____

_____

_____

CHAPTER FOUR
LIVE AT A SACRED PACE

"The real voyage of discovery consists not in seeking new landscapes, but in having new eyes."
—Marcel Proust

"I have gone out to find myself. If I should return before I get back, please tell me to wait."
—Anonymous

"...but the fact that I have leeway, that nothing need be forced, makes the difference."
—May Sarton

"Adventure is not something you must travel to find...it is something you take with you."
—Diane Ackerman

What's the Hurry?

One morning, hurtling from my desk toward the photo-copier, I passed a roomful of colleagues just about to start a meeting. There was someone I needed to talk to. I saw immediately that he wasn't among them, but I put my head in the door before they could begin, and in a very loud, urgent voice, I said, "Has anyone seen David?"

There was a moment of stunned incomprehension, which to my amazement, quickly dissolved into table-thumping laughter. My comic timing must have been impeccable, because the whole room was soon helpless repeating what I had said and generally behaving like the pig-ignorant fools other people seem to be when the joke is at our expense. I looked back at them blankly, the truth dawning as I looked. "Has anyone seen David" might seem an innocuous question in most organizations, but I happened to be the only David who worked under that particular roof. I realized the forlorn and public stupidity of my request and forced myself, after a wide-eyed moment, to laugh with them. Inside, I was dying.

I was looking for David, all right, and I couldn't find him. In fact, I hadn't seen him for a long time. I was looking for a David who had disappeared under a swampy morass of stress and speed.

So confesses David Whyte in his book, *Crossing the Unknown Sea: Work as a Pilgrimage to Identity.*

My Addiction to Hurry

Getting back into the swing of things was a post-vacation ritual to which I was accustomed, but this time things were different. I felt an unusual uneasiness about resuming my regular schedule. I loved being back home with family and friends; I loved my work; I loved where we lived; what was wrong? Discontent led to confusion; confusion led to grief. What saddened me so in the summer of 1998 was the sense of a pending loss. What I feared losing was a more relaxed living pace that I had fallen into, or that had fallen into me.

I noticed it during a cruise with my wife to Alaska. I was awed by the vastness of the waterways we traveled. I had seen great bodies of water before, but for the first time in my life I was in great masses of water for days. From our large window, I marveled at all the water; it didn't seem to end, and I thought that it was as deep as it was wide. The glaciers stopped me: towering masses that were not green or brown but white. Louisiana, my home state, had not afforded me such sightings. Perhaps the most astounding vision of all for me was the streams rolling down the sides of mountains. Not just seeing them, but hearing them brought me to extended pauses and complete stops. While I expected that the trip to Alaska would be a memorable one, I did not expect that it would move me so.

As I thought about it more and more, I began to realize that my summer sadness was connected to my Alaskan vacation. It wasn't so much a missing of the special places but the extended pauses and complete stops the places had inspired.

Up to this point, I had lived most of my life as though haste was a moral virtue. It wasn't just about setting and achieving worthy goals, but it was about doing so as soon as possible. In my personal and professional life, I lived as though fast was faithful and hurry was holy. I stacked accelerated accomplishments on top of each other with no small satisfaction. That summer, a subversive idea challenged my satisfaction and began transforming my life. The idea is this: *Life doesn't have to be fast to be fun and fulfilling.*

The Sacred Pace

Sacred Pace is an alternative to living life in a hurry. It is doing so by making an intentional effort to see more clearly the ordinary and the extraordinary, listen more carefully to sounds and silences, and think more deeply, especially about those ideas and thoughts that stimulate new growth and positive change. I discuss each of these elements in my earlier book, *Addicted to Hurry: Spiritual Strategies for Slowing Down* and an E-book, *The Savoring Pace: 52 Ways to Slow Down and Enjoy Your Life.* Since both works are readily available at my website www. kirkbjones.com and other online outlets, I will not repeat here what I've previously said. Suffice it for me to say here that in the seven years that have elapsed since my first writings on hurry-addiction, the need to cultivate a sacred pace has never been more important. If anything, the hurry-problem has gotten worse. And, we continue to bless chronic speed with religious affirmation. I have a picture in my files of a young man walking alone with a shirt reading, "Jesus is coming back; look busy."

Perhaps the primary culprit regarding hurry's sustained hold on us is our easy acceptance of multi-tasking. We have gotten used to doing multiple things simultaneously, as fast as possible. It has become our way. Yet, the price we pay in errors made, surface relationships, and muted creativity is, I believe, too high. Sometimes I imagine having a special day to cause us to wake up and envision a richer pace of living characterized by lavish amounts of awareness, patience, and peace. I suggest calling such a day, **One-Thing-at-a-Time-Day.** This would be a day in which all persons would be encouraged to resist all multi-tasking, and focus on doing one thing at a time, calmly, deliberately, and where possible, with great pleasure. That wouldn't be so bad, would it?

Don't Fall to All

The New Revised Standard Version of Luke's Gospel, Chapter 8, verses 40-42, offers the following passage:

Now when Jesus returned, the crowd welcomed him, for they were all waiting for him. Just then there came a man named Jairus, a leader of the synagogue. He fell at Jesus' feet and begged him to come to his house, for he had an only daughter, about twelve years old, who was dying.

"They were all waiting for him." You bet they were. Jesus was heading back to his home region after a rather noteworthy evangelistic crusade. Along with preaching captivating sermon-stories, Jesus had allegedly, through the power of his spoken word, halted a storm and cured a man possessed by demons. Is it any wonder that Jesus would have trouble sneaking back into town unnoticed?

Chances are some in the crowd had needs of their own, none of which rivaled the great challenges that Jesus faced with the storm and the demons. Surely, Jesus would have a moment to hand out a few minor miracles. Maybe others in the welcoming party just came to watch, and perhaps shake his hand and say, "Way to go, Jesus!"

What I want you to note from the text is that though "all" waited for him for whatever reasons, Jesus responded to the request of just one, Jairus, whose daughter was deathly ill. Though confronted and surrounded with tens if not hundreds of legitimate concerns, demands, and expectations, Jesus gave himself permission to choose one matter for the moment.

Single-mindedness is an endangered practice. We are conditioned to do multiple things at a time. It has become our way of life, our oppressive obsession. What a liberating blessing of grace and space, to give ourselves permission to choose one over all, more often than not.

Slowing Down to Exercise Your Creative Response Muscle

Living at a slower pace gives us the time to be less negatively reactive and more positively active in our lives. Chronic hurry takes away important spaces, times, and rests that we may use to identify and create creative positive responses for any situation.

Rushing puts us at the mercy of our first non-reflective reactive response. We end up acting in ways that we often regret later. This is particularly true when we are blindsided and momentarily upset by something said or done to us. Though it seems irresistible and natural, we do not have to be carried away by our first feelings in the face of things that are upsetting to us. The point here is not to condemn feelings of anger or rage. Being alive means feeling such emotions. Such emotions have their rightful place in our lives.

The point is this: If we practice pausing and using our creative response muscle, we do not have to be controlled by any circumstance or situation.

Your creative response muscle is your God-given capacity to control your thoughts, feelings, and actions. It is your sacred skill to carve out the best from the worst. It is your divine ability to see and seize opportunity in disappointment.

Here is a "Declaration of Creative Responsibility" to assist you in exercising your creative response muscle:

> I control my thoughts, feelings, and actions.
>
> I can't control what happens, but I can control my response to what happens.
>
> When I am upset, I pause to set up a positive creative response.

Learning to Live with the Undone

I am writing this on the morning of December 13, 2008. It is leaf pickup day in our neighborhood, the day the town sanitation workers collect leaves from neighbors who have dutifully collected them for transport. Today, I am not one of those neighbors. I have had the chore scheduled for weeks, and have looked forward to the annual ritual. In the past, we have paid others to perform the task, but, quite frankly I have enjoyed doing it, especially when our children were younger and we made it a family project. Well, there is only one teenager in the house now, JoJo, and let's just say lawn work is not her calling. So, the truck has passed by no less than three times this morning, as if to be teasing and taunting me about the task that was left undone.

But, it's OK.

It has been a busy two weeks, including teaching two classes, leading weekly religious services, performing funerals, fulfilling family commitments, and oh yes, concluding two major writing projects. In the mix of things, the leaves did not get picked up.

So be it.

I have learned and am continuing to learn to gracefully live with the undone. While in the past, I may have gotten up early this morning to make sure that the sanitation workers had some contribution from 39 Stoughton Street, I remained in bed and enjoyed an extended Saturday morning respite, cuddled next to my wife. The leaves never crossed my mind.

I know by reviewing my work over the past month that I am not a disorganized, negligent, or lazy person. At the very worst, I simply over-scheduled, not allowing sufficient time and margin for all the tasks I planned and unplanned, yet important obligations. I have discovered that the best remedy for such a moment is noticing, and gracing myself. Guilt is no longer a part of the prescription. So let the trucks roll past my house, three or 300 times. Our leaves will not be aboard this day.

And, that's OK.

Glory is Free

Sitting outside,

hearing and feeling

strong New England night wind

blowing through the trees.

I think and thank:

This grand glory is free.

—KBJ

A Request

Hurry,

please

hurry on

out of my life.

—KBJ

Peace Rinse

There are few things in life

more deeply,

mysteriously,

and soulfully

satisfying

than

simply

easing back

and

listening

to the rain.

—KBJ

Exaltation before Expectation

Have you ever shed

glad grateful tears for a moment?

Not for what the moment held

but for the grand grace of your holding

another moment.

—KBJ

Carry One Day

Carry one day.

Put yesterday down.

Don't pick up tomorrow.

Carry one day.

—KBJ

7 Sacred Pace Affirmations:

1.
I live at the speed of peace.

2.
What I need most is not in the race; it's in the grace.

3.
I will walk in step with my angels.

4.
Hurry has lost its hold on me.

5.
I will take my time so that time can take me.

6.
Peace is my pacesetter.

7.
ASAP means "As Savoring As Possible."

Personal Reflection/Group Discussion Questions

Why are we always in a hurry?

_____

_____

_____

_____

_____

What are the perceived benefits of hurry?

_____

_____

_____

_____

_____

How does chronic hurry harm us?

_____

_____

_____

_____

_____

What are the actual benefits of living at a sacred pace?

_____

_____

_____

_____

_____

Identify five ways you can cultivate a more patient and peaceful living pace.

_____

_____

_____

_____

_____

Personal Journal Page

Affirmations:

_____

_____

_____

_____

_____

Questions:

_____

_____

_____

_____

Reflections:

_____

_____

_____

_____

CHAPTER FIVE
CLAIM YOUR INNER CALM

"Then I enter a place of not-thinking, not-remembering, not-wanting."
    —Mary Oliver

"Silence is the soul's break for freedom."
    — David Whyte

"So the darkness shall be the light, and the stillness the dancing."
    —T.S. Eliot

"B Still"
    —License Plate on Car in Randolph, MA

"A certain kind of peace depends on resolution to exist, but pure peace exists within dissonance. It is peace before, after, and in the storm."
— KBJ

Stillness: A Sweet Summer Surprise

The summer had come and gone and I felt frustrated and restless. In just a few weeks it would be time to begin another academic year of teaching and another season of speaking on the road. The summer, my 50th, was to be my time of deeper than usual respite and reflection. I planned accordingly, but then life and a lack of insistence on my part had unplanned. Before I knew it, an extended period of relaxation had become a broken break. In a last bid to salvage what I could from my lost Sabbath, I thought to take advantage of an opportunity to spend a week alone at a retreat center. The little yellow house on the backside of the center's forested grounds and the lake next to it saved me.

Sometimes thirst is enough. I received a blessing of deep peace during my few days on the lake, maybe because I wanted it so. Mornings were spent walking along the small sandy beach and wading in the water. Afternoons saw me seated on rocks in the forest looking around and within. Evenings, I lounged in the house in utter silence, broken only by the soft Jazz I brought to join me. It was a time of emptying all burdens of worry, and abiding in spaces the poet Mary Oliver calls, "not thinking, not remembering, and not wanting." In the 11th hour, my summer Sabbath had been salvaged. I had touched what a great disciple of stillness, Howard Thurman, called "the physical and mental cessation of inner churning."

Just as I was about to break out into full grief for my having to go away from my getaway, I discovered that God had saved the best for last. I sought to chronicle the surprise blessing in my final journal entry of that week:

Stillness, inner peace, is not a vacation. Peace is a lifestyle. You have a lake, trails, a forest within you that you can go to anytime you desire. You do not have to go away to go away; just go within.

In that moment, I felt that I didn't have to leave the most important thing I had discovered at the lake, deep inner calm, behind; I could take it with me. Suddenly, a new awareness had hold of me: *I carry my calm inside of me all the time.* This knowledge caused me to recall words that had fallen into my consciousness during a personal morning devotional moment earlier in the year:

Where Love Lives

If you can be

still enough

long enough

there is a place within

on the other side of silence

where love lives.

—KBJ

Overcoming our Suspicion of Stillness

In order to observe more inner calm and peace, we must come to terms with our conscious and unconscious negative valuations of stillness. For example, we associate stillness with mischief. If young children are too quiet in a home, an alarm may go off inside of us: "What in the world are they up to?" At other times, stillness is used as a punishment: "Sit down and don't you move a muscle!" Sometimes we punish persons who have offended us by giving them "the silent treatment." Another example of a negative perception of stillness is our discomfort with extended pauses in conversation. Finally, we may associate quiet with trying personal life situations. I remember a seminary student linking her uneasiness with stillness with "the calm just before the storm" of another abusive assault from her father.

Though sometimes painful, identifying ways in which stillness has been negatively experienced is a way of preparing stillness to wear new garments, to take on greater positive meaning and value in our still-thisty lives.

Cultivating Stillness-Desire

We receive what we deeply desire; what we focus on is what expands in our lives. Consequently, you will not realize more stillness and the resulting peace of mind and soul in your life unless you truly want it. Warning: *Given that our society promotes noise and busyness, you will have to develop your desirability in a hostile environment.* It is possible to increase your "want-ability factor" by periodically reminding yourself of the amazing life-transforming benefits of stillness. Here are a few such benefits attested to by, not only writers and religious leaders, but persons in varying walks of life I have encountered in seminars and workshops around the country:

1. Calm

2. Soul Refreshing

3. Hearing God's Voice

4. Acceptance

5. Release

6. Insight

7. Clarity

8. Soulfulness

9. Surprises

10. Originality

11. Connection to God, Self, Nature, and Others

12. Contentment

13. Elation

14. Lavish Grace

15. Inner Spaciousness

16. Courage to Face Fear

17. Creative Energy

18. Noticing More

19. Patience

20. Stretching

Take a moment to reflect on each stillness-blessing and its meaning for you, past, present, and future.

Peace-Pockets: A New Stillness Ritual

Peace-pockets are 5-15 minute intentional intervals throughout the day for spiritual, mental and spiritual respite and renewal. During your peace-pocket time, you may listen to soft music, watch a burning candle, pay attention to your breathing, allow your mind to wander free, or give it the freedom to not wander anywhere or think of anything at all. The goal is to be "off" for a moment. The more experience you build, the better you will become at observing your peace-pockets. Here are four things to remember as you create your unique and soulfully refreshing peace-pockets:

1. **Permission**. If you don't value your calm, no one else will. You have to become convinced of the meaning and value for peace in your own life. You have to become persuaded that you are a better person with peace than without peace. Convince yourself that stillness leads to peace, peace leads to clarity, and clarity leads to creativity. Should you begin to feel guilty and selfish about making more time for nothing, dare to believe that the deeper selfishness is not giving yourself such time. As long as you remain "crazy busy" you insure that the world, including those nearest and dearest to you, will never behold you at your finest. That would be selfish.

2. **Planning.** Schedule daily and weekly times of stillness, and be open to the unscheduled graces of free time to simply be. Planning them with the same intent that you plan your work signals to your consciousness, and just as importantly your unconscious mind, that claiming your inner calm is as important to you as anything else in your life.

3. **Practice.** Don't just plan your mini-respite, live it. Real change involves more than knowing you need to change, wanting to, and planning to. As valuable as they are, authentic change transcends awareness and desire. Real change is actually choosing to be different, to live different. And, sustaining true change involves trusting your transformation beyond all fear and suffering.

4. **Personhood.** Know that having regular periods of stillness helps you to remember that you are infinitely more than what you do. You are God's "fabulous you" apart from any accomplishment or achievement. God cannot love you any more than God loves you right now, not because of anything you have done or will do.

You Are Already in Peace; Peace is Already in You

If you don't mind, please take a deep breath. Go ahead; breathe in deeply. Hold it. Now, exhale. Do it again. Breathe in deeply; hold; release your breath. And, just one more time, completely inhale; exhale completely.

Hopefully, you have just experienced several seconds of complete inner calm: a piece of peace.

I am guessing that you were so focused on taking, holding, and releasing air that you did not think to think about anything else. Not thinking about *anything* allowed you to be free of *everything*, including all anxiety, fear, and worry. Inner peace is not an elusive blissful state achievable only by the highly spiritual. It is all around you all the time. You're standing in it; it is standing in you. The arduous effort of stillness is simple awareness.

Because inner peace is God and God is everywhere, all the peace you will ever want or need is already present around and inside of you. Similarly, all the love you will ever want or need is already present around and inside of you.

One of the biggest impediments to experiencing inner peace is the perception that we are always so far from it. Always, you are much closer to peace than you think. Always, peace within is never more than a small still moment away.

A Direct Path to Peace

Stillness is the most direct path to the peace that is always around and within us. I believe this is true for two reasons: the listening and releasing power of stillness.

Stillness calls us to *listen*. Stillness allows us to better hear and feel the peace that is the sacred undertone of everything that was, is, and ever will be. Thus, stillness enables us to more readily pick up peace: the everlasting signal of serenity that is always emanating from God. I believe this divine undisturbed peace has never been nor can ever be diminished. Just as important for us is the fact that this peace envelopes us. We can only know this to be true by listening and leaning in to its truth.

By the way, by using the very same letters, "listen" spells "silent."

Secondly, I believe stillness is the most direct path to peace because it calls us to *release*. A moment ago when I asked you to practice breathing, half of your action involved exhaling or letting go. That was and is always a risk on our part. But it is the risk that enriches. Only through releasing breath do we make room for fresh breaths of air. *Releasing is refreshing.* Similarly, by facilitating a relinquishing of life's stresses, silence opens us up to fresh peace, God's continuing pure peace undiluted by the troubles of this or any other world.

If peace is in God then it is ever-present. Our challenge, therefore, is not to make peace as in create peace, but to more consciously, intentionally, and regularly practice peace. Our challenge is to make peace with peace, to make peace with the peace that already is, and always will be. Inner spaciousness and peace breeds outer spaciousness and peace.

Go Deeper

Sometimes during moments of silence and introspection images will fall and form in my mental space. They are unforced and just arise from my unconscious or some other place. When this first started to happen, I was jolted because the pictures are so impressionable and lifelike. If I let myself go, it's as if I really am in the place that has fallen into my consciousness. I have learned to let go and lean into such graced moments.

One morning while easing into a time of intentionally not thinking about anything at all, an image of a pit formed in my mind. It was deep and dark, but yet enchantingly inviting somehow. Before I could think not to, I jumped. Down I went farther and farther until I landed, and began feeling the walls of this new place. An unseen camera seemed to zoom in on my presence in this deeper place. As I stood immersed in inquiry, slowly the image melted away. In its place, two words sounded, "Go Deeper."

For the next several moments, my appointed time of not thinking about anything was warmly interspersed with provocative, yet non-intrusive word arrangements, including the following:

How do I go deeper in my life?

Where am I feeling compelled to go deeper?

Slow down; Stop; Look; Listen; Question

Depth, Richness, Understanding

Deep, Deepening Knowledge and Wisdom

It seems to me that one of the things we sacrifice in our hurried busyness is depth of living. Somehow doing a lot fast is leaving us empty and lost. What if there is greater wealth in going deeper with the things we have than in acquiring more? What if the key to happiness is not relentless acquisition but deepening awareness?

What is the good of having anything at all, if you don't know what it is that you truly have?

Stillness and Clarity

In her beautifully profound, *The Secret Life of Bees*, Sue Monk Kidd includes the following insightful passage:

Every human being on the face of the earth has a steel plate in his head, but if you lie down now and then and get as still as you can, it will slide open like elevator doors, letting in all the secret thoughts that have been standing around so patiently, pushing the button for the ride to the top. The real troubles in life happen when those doors stay closed for too long.

Our steel plate can keep us from perceiving and owning our deep desires: what it is we truly want for ourselves. Understand that when you are still, your steel plate of ignorance and confusion is sliding open, allowing you access to the truths that will help you move on in your life with confident clarity.

Turn Your Buttons Off

You control your response to everything, including your reaction to people who know all too well how to get under your skin. They know where your last nerve is, and how to get there. If you genuinely want to end their reign over your emotions, resist the rising pressure when they press your buttons. Grace someone in this way and you take away their power to control your emotions. Easier said than done, but start your mastery of this ability by imagining it being possible. And, then desire what you imagine.

Practice turning your buttons off before stressful encounters. Decide beforehand that the usual words and ways of upsetting you no longer work. Imagine yourself, instead, being patient and gracious with others no matter what they say or do. To enhance your growth in this powerful new ability, see yourself having wells of grace and mercy that are constantly being replenished by God's inexhaustible love.

As you turn your buttons off and discover new creative ways of relating with others, you are not becoming a doormat; you are opening new doors of interpersonal skill and empowerment that will bless your life, others, and the world.

Stillness, Exploration, and Empowerment

I enjoy playing sports, strategy, and adventure video games. The latter is enjoyable, in part, because of the surprise finds. For me, the best games are the ones that encourage you to explore broadly, and reward you with the discovery of valuable items that only people actively and vastly searching will have a chance at finding. Usually what is found enhances the finder: more health, strength, or power.

Exploration-Desire is one of our greatest gifts. Questions are indicators of not just life, but lavish life. When life launches out beyond itself, it expands and enriches itself. This is sacred stuff. For all we know, all of creation may have commenced the moment wonder wandered. (What are you wondering about these days? In what new directions are you wandering?)

Stillness allows time for us to wonder and wander

about this and that. It offers us a chance to examine and explore our world, especially the world within: our thoughts, feelings, perceptions and motivations. Constant engagement in a nonstop society leaves little time for reflection. Yet reflection is most essential amid an unceasing onslaught of choices, demands, and expectations. Time to assess, define, and focus has never been more important to our species. Without such time we end up living lifted and lofted, from here to there, with no enlivening sense of purpose and fulfillment.

Stillness offers us the opportunity to glimpse within, and consequently intentionally and mindfully forge connections and fashion creations that are the matter of truly astounding and astonishing living: living up to God's highest expectations and not down to our lowest ones. In the stillness, we flex and stretch our reflective muscles, developing our sacred super powers of self-knowledge and self-actualization. In the stillness, we gain a greater sense of who we are and what we are capable of at our greatest. The fully empowered self is the self, found and free.

Being Still to Connect with You

Thinking is wonderful. Feeling is wonderful. But, we are more than what we think and what we feel. To get a sense of your greater, deeper limitless self, you must experience existence beyond human thought and feeling. In fact, this experience of your expanded spaciousness is not new to you. We all derive from God's heart, our true home, our "spirit-base." We are spiritual beings having a human experience.

When we still our thoughts and take leave of our

feelings, in that moment we go home. We experience the deep and wide expanse that God enjoys in every moment. That God-moment becomes our God-moment, our existence as God's child in all of our infinite finery and fullness.

Stillness is a proven best entryway to our larger sense of self. As we allow ourselves to become still more often, we learn more about our inner spaciousness and dynamism. The great tragedy is that we rarely sense the spiritual largesse about us. What if we could know our greater spiritual essence more keenly and access it more frequently? What if this great and vast reservoir of spiritual strength could influence our thoughts, feelings, and intuitions continually? Stillness makes this possible. It allows us ready access to our spirit-base. As we become more familiar with our greater soul-self, it will feel less foreign to us, and living within its terrain will be so natural that it won't be second nature to us, but first nature.

Get Hold of You

In his wonderful autobiography, *Treat it Gentle*, legendary jazz clarinetist, Sidney Bechet, makes the following observation about the difference between bands that played just what they knew and bands that played what they knew and more:

You know, when you learn something, you can go just so far. When you've finished that, there's not much else you can do unless you know how to get hold of something inside you that isn't learned. It has to be there inside you without any need of learning. The band that played what it knew, it didn't have enough. In the end it would get confused; it was finished. And the people, they could tell.

The phrase "get hold of something inside you" intrigues me. It reminds me of words Jesus kept saying over and over again to people: "The Kingdom of God is within you." What if spirituality is not so much about grasping for things that are outside us, but more about grabbing hold to things that are within us?

Stay in Tune with Your Inner Voice

The pressures to conform, settle, and yield are so ruthless that it takes tenacious desire to hear and honor one's own inner voice and callings. Save spaces for solitude; don't be afraid of silence. Observing solitude and silence in the margins of busy living is a way of remaining true to our depths, to who we really are when all the roles are set aside, and all the masks come off. When we are constantly busy, no matter how important the tasks, we risk never really knowing who we are, what we want, and where we are going.

Take time to be still in order to know: *to become genuinely familiar with your vast inner wealth.* Staying in tune with your inner voice and remaining true to who you are should not be seen as selfish acts. Being true to your soulful uniqueness is your highest praise to God, and your best offering to the world.

Stillness Mental Clearing Exercise

Here are three questions for stillness reflection and recreation: What assumptions contribute to my vision of reality? How might changing my assumptions change my vision of reality? What new choices can I create for myself simply by changing my assumptions? Of course these questions are based on three grand assumptions:

(1) Our vision of reality is based on our assumptions. (2) When we make new assumptions, we can create new choices. (3) When we create new choices, we change and transform our lives.

Regularly, take time to open wide all the doors and windows of your familiar commitments and presumptions, to let in the sunlight and fresh air of new perspectives.

Be Still to Distill What Matters Most

Are you a slave to multitasking? Too often we end up not only trying to do it all, but trying to do it all at the same time. One way out of this unhealthy habit is to become more proficient at prioritizing. Here is a three-step method for extracting or distilling what's most important from all that we think is important:

1. Create a mini to-do list. Try to limit this initial list to a maximum of seven tasks, but don't assign numbers to any of them. Once your list is done, set it aside.

2. Still your thinking. Find a comfortable place and sit as quietly as you can for a minimum of five minutes. Do not think of your list or anything else. One way to accomplish this is to focus on something empty; e.g. an empty cup or vase. If thoughts enter your mind, simply ease or wave them on. The vacuum created by your not thinking is your space of fresh clarity for what needs to be done next.

3. Rank the items on your mini to-do list. Be guided by what has naturally risen to the top of your mind in your moment of mental distilling.

Pay Attention to the Things that Quiet You

Perhaps you have been reading this chapter and thinking, "It sounds good, but I don't know if I can do it. I don't know if I can develop the practice of being still. The truth is, chances are you have already started developing the practice. Think about the things in your life that tend to slow you down and quiet your spirit. In fact, take a moment to list seven such things in the space provided below.

Things that Quiet Me:

1. _____

2. _____

3. _____

4. _____

5. _____

6. _____

7. _____

Here are seven things that quiet me:

1. <u>"Little" Jimmy Scott's Singing</u> Jimmy Scott is a magnificent Jazz singer, still singing at his own unique soulfully slow, sweet pace in his 80s.

2. <u>A Burning Candle</u>

3. <u>Running Water</u>

4. <u>Sunsets</u>

5. Clear Skies

6. Morning Light in Shaded Trees

7. Rain

I consider my quieting realities my "Professors of Stillness." I invite you to grant the same status to the things that easily and naturally bring you to a place of peace. Attend more of their classes; don't ever graduate from their tutelage.

Lao-Tzu said, "Be still and the whole world surrenders." The world that we need to surrender most to stillness is our crazy-busy existence of endless anxiety and non-existent peace. *Dare to claim your inner calm.*

Lounging in God's Grace

God, help me to be still

to lounge

in Your grace

and listen

to Your song,

and to hear my song

in Yours.

—KBJ

7 Inner Calm Affirmations:

1.
It's the nothingness that sets up the something-ness.

2.
No sitting; no soaring.

3.
Settling down in my inner world sends calm to my outer world.

4.
Inner spaciousness and peace breeds outer spaciousness and peace.

5.
I relax full and free in God's love and grace.

6.
I will be still and sip slowly from God's cup of grace.

7.
I find love, fulfillment, and joy in stillness.

Personal Reflection/Group Discussion Questions

What was your experience of silence and solitude during your childhood?

_____

_____

_____

_____

_____

Are you/we afraid of stillness? Why? Why not?

_____

_____

_____

_____

_____

Why is stillness difficult to cultivate?

_____

_____

_____

_____

How can we welcome stillness more?

_____

_____

_____

_____

_____

Identify five stillness strategies that you will attempt to practice over the next several months.

_____

_____

_____

_____

_____

Personal Journal Page

Affirmations:

_____

_____

_____

_____

_____

Questions:

_____

_____

_____

_____

_____

Reflections:

_____

_____

_____

_____

CHAPTER SIX
BALANCE ASPIRATION
WITH CONTENTMENT

"It is well with my soul."
— Horatio Spafford

"He needed to go someplace where he could rise to the occasion of his own life."
— Valerie Boyd

"As the wind loves to call things to dance,
May your gravity be lightened by grace."
— John O'Donohue

"One more thing that you should bring is a flag to plant at each new summit. There you'll rest and watch it wave, and feel good about how far you've come."
— Suzanne Willis Zoglio

"We need to float in the waters of contentment instead of always scaling mountains of accomplishment."
　—KBJ

Going, Going, Going, Gone

It happened suddenly and without warning. One moment, I was up preaching during the first night of a week-long revival meeting, and in the next moment I was standing speechless before a stunned congregation. It wasn't that I'd lost my ability to speak. Thankfully, I was not suffering a stroke. That night, now over 20 years ago, I was just too tired to say another word.

Preaching since the age of 12, I had preached through fatigue before. In fact, some of the most memorable sermons had come when I'd pushed myself to stand and preach through tiredness and sometimes even sickness. I'd learned how to wave off fatigue, and rely on hidden energy reserves and the Holy Spirit to pull me through. I had even developed a visualization process to help me preach when low on energy. Before rising up to speak, I would imagine an angel on either side of where I'd stand to preach. They would be there to bear me up. There was something spiritually dynamic and heroic about it all.

But, that night was different; there were no heroics. I did not have the strength to speak, draw from energy reserves, or imagine angelic support. All I had the strength to do was say the following words to those who had come out to the revival service: "I can't go on." The revivalist needed to be revived.

Unchecked Aspiration

My experience that night was my introduction to burn-out. In my early 30s then, my life had been a rapid ascent to pulpit, college, theological school, and the pastorate. Through it all, I relished planning and achieving at an accelerated pace. I wanted to accomplish as much as I could as soon as I could for God, church, and world, and for me. I loved achieving. I enjoyed feeling ambitious, and feeding my ambition. The fact that my work was "God's work" fueled my flames of aspiration even more.

I did not suspect there could or would be a problem with my fixation on ambition until my pulpit wake-up call. In the days and months that followed, I began to understand that I needed to make some radical adjustments if I was going to live healthy and whole. The primary adjustments have been mental. I now believe that unchecked ambition is deadly. Drivenness, even towards the most laudable ends, jeopardizes our emotional, physical, and spiritual health. Moreover, our work and overall offering to the world is compromised and threatened. You are no use to anyone—dead.

I don't believe the answer is a full-scale attack on ambition and achievement. As I heard legendary preacher Gardner C. Taylor say once, "Where would we be if no one wanted to do anything?" Thank God for the desire to soar. Yet, in order to insure that our soaring does not result in crash landings, we need to balance achievement with a comparable reality. That reality is contentment.

Feeling the Breeze of Contentment: Doing Takes a Vacation

I am writing this outside on a breezy summer morning. Writing indoors today would be a sin, no matter what I would say. Our yard is surrounded by trees, and so each time a breeze comes through, I not only feel the refreshing sensation on my skin, but I hear a soft roaring: nature's applause as the wind glides through the leaves. It is a wonderful feeling. The fact that I have learned to pay attention to the breeze and appreciate its effects on me is an indication of progress. Such things as feeling a cool breeze, walking along, and looking up at the sky are now as meaningful to me as any desired goal. When I am enjoying these leisurely moments the most, I am not thinking of anything I have to do. Doing takes a vacation; I am simply being, and thoroughly being in and enjoying the moment for the moment's sake and for my soul's sake.

I imagine contentment as the gentle breeze of feeling that all is well. It is completely free of reaching and striving. When we are content, we are in a moment of not needing or wanting anything. To be content is to feel satisfied with what is and what you have. "More" is not only not needed, it is not even considered. Full contentment is a combination of love, peace, and joy, and when you are in it and it is in you, nothing else matters.

Happiness vs. Contentment: Fulfillment beyond Your Smile

When told that a renowned video gaming designer's

goal was to see a smile on players' faces, fellow designer, David Cage, responded, "My goal is to see an emotion on the players' faces whether it is happiness, disgust, fear, or tears. The worst thing would be to see no expression at all."

After some initial resistance (Why not want to see a smile first and foremost on the faces of gamers?), I came to agree with Cage, and modified my endorsement of happiness as the ultimate end of gaming design and life. Sure, being happy is a laudable goal; who wants to be sad? Yet, focusing too much on happiness can diminish our appreciation for many other comparably splendid but usually underrated emotions of life, like astonishment, wonder, and at times, even fear. Think about the moments in life when you may not have been smiling, but you were engaged, learning, searching, and growing. Though maybe painfully so, you were undeniably alive.

Perhaps, *active-appreciative-awareness* is the high calling of life, higher than happiness for sure. Moreover, *active-appreciative-awareness*, being awake and thankful, it seems to me, holds the stuff of contentment: a continual undergirding abiding sense of grace, through it all—not just the happy times.

Enjoying Evening Breeze

In this moment

it's not just how

the breeze feels on me,

but how it sounds

gliding through the leaves

fancying them too,

before they fall.

—KBJ

The Dance between Aspiration and Contentment

It is important to not see aspiration and contentment as enemies of each other. Instead, see them as dancing together, exchanging motions of leading and following. Aspiration feeds and fuels contentment; contentment feeds and fuels aspiration.

Part of our feeling content involves feeling good about having worthy goals, and being on our way towards achieving them, as well as having achieved some already. Accomplishment makes us feel good. We do ourselves a disservice when we don't take the time to savor our achievements. Part of what leads to job bitterness is not taking the time to savor a job well-done. We miss much when we miss the muchness of our lives as they are right now. Feeling good about accomplishment nurtures self-esteem and self-confidence. Such contentment-laced aspiration offers sacred momentum not to just live, but to live with sustained purpose and continual joy. Aspiration and savoring aspiration-fulfillment adds to our sense of satisfaction with ourselves, and with life.

To feel content is one of the best things we can do for our ambitions. To continually live in striving mode, no matter how laudable the enterprise, leaves us feeling tired and empty. So many people can attest to the sudden onset of the dreaded "is this all there is feeling." This is the feeling that drops in on us when we begin to wonder why everything we have worked for doesn't provide us with the fulfillment we anticipated. What a jolt it is to have everything we've ever wanted, and feel sadly and strangely empty inside.

The solution to an uneasy feeling of dismay and dissatisfaction amidst the presence of plenty is to learn how to practice contentment. Contentment satisfies our yearning hearts. Moreover, contentment, taking moments to pause and more fully appreciate now without reaching for the future, insures that we get the rest moments that a rejuvenated spirit requires.

Living the Balance between Aspiration and Contentment

It is one thing to experience theoretical harmony between our honorable and deliberate striving for more and our being intentionally satisfied with what we have. It is another thing to actually put this harmonious relationship into practice. With this daunting but doable challenge in mind, here are nine ways to creatively aspire from a place of joyful, soulful and peaceful contentment, nine ways to become the CEO of **YOUR PEACE**:

1. **Y**ield to what is. Much suffering is caused by our wanting things to be different from what they are. Dreams, hopes, and expectations are vital to optimal living, but we can over-fixate on them. You know you are over-fixating when your sense of happiness is always linked to a future manifestation. Cultivate the habit of realizing happiness in the present moment irrespective of what the future does or does not offer.

2. **O**wn your incompletions. Often we setup ourselves for inevitable let-down by overbooking the day. Our planned schedule can stress us out before undertaking task number one. We may manage on the front-end of the day by scheduling less. An effective back-end of the day strategy is learning to live with the undone. Allow yourself to be at peace with what you had planned to do but were not able to get to that day. Tell yourself that the matter will be handled sufficiently soon enough, and that the extra time to address it may even provide for a greater solution to the challenge. A great day is not one in which you've done everything. You have a great day by giving the day a great you. A great you is a content and satisfied you.

3. **U**nhook what you do from who you are. We are all guilty of it: upon meeting someone, immediately asking them, "What do you do?" It is an innocent

cultural common conversation starter. Innocent though it may be, it helps to perpetuate the lie that what we do is the most important feature of what we are. It is not. The most important feature of who we are is who we are apart from roles, expectations, and obligations. We are not what we do; what we do is but one expression of who we are. Aspire and perform from a place of pre-established contentment, so that your personhood does not depend on your productivity.

4. **R**est in the unknown. Contentment doesn't just depend on rest as we discussed in the first chapter, but it depends on resting in the unknown. Being able to rest when we are not sure of where we are or what's up ahead is a challenge. One of the ways we can meet the challenge is by cultivating a less menacing understanding of the unknown. Once, when I saw the word "fun" showcased in an unusually bright and brilliant way, the following sentiment spilled in and out of my mind: *The "un" in "fun" stands for the uncharted, the undiscovered, and the unknown. There is delight in adventure.*

5. **P**ractice Stopping. Busyness is the source of much modern discontent. It is not that we are so busy, but many of us are addicted to being so busy. Not being busy places us in a state of temporary discomfort. Such a state is necessary however, because learning to stop and hold our energy is a crucial tool for cultivating contentment. Stopping is risky, because it suggests that who we are, where we are, and what we have in the moment is enough. And, that is exactly the sentiment we convey to our souls and

our souls convey to us when we dare to stop and relax in a moment of deep contentment.

6. **E**njoy what you do. Contentment is not just about not doing, it is about doing with joy. As best you can, when you can, take joy into your tasks, whatever the task. Sometimes joy is natural, unforced and free flowing. At other times, joy needs to be primed and pumped. Whether flowing or manufactured through effort, joy is a sure contentment enhancer. Everything goes better with joy.

7. **A**void the curse of the competent. The curse of the competent is being good at many things, so good that many persons are constantly requesting your services. The ultimate bite of the curse is constant consent: an inability to say, "No" when one's plate is already overloaded. Learn to excel without always expecting to be and trying to be all things to all people. Sometimes you will not have the support or understanding of others in a particular pursuit; all you will have is the burning of an inner yearning. But, that is all you will need.

8. **C**ease trying to measure up to others. One of the ways we fall into work discontent is by trying to keep up with people who do not have a healthy life-work balance. Trying to keep up with others will turn work-joy into work-dread. Be satisfied with your best. Your best is your optimal creativity at a sacred pace. It is your most splendid offering to the world without sacrificing your physical, mental, and spiritual health.

9. **E**stablish a daily/weekly review. Become accus-

tomed to seeing yourself in the role of observer and monitoring your life. When it comes to contentment, this means diligently noting those moments when you are content, and having a growing knowledge of the activities and non-activities that make you feel most alive. Don't leave your contentment to chance. Direct, record, and evaluate contentment in your life. Note that your goal is not perfection, but contentment. Besides, I believe classical pianist, Sherman Russell, is right not just about music but about composing and playing a life, when he says, "Perfection is too mundane, brittle, uptight for those who would make music the way God makes trees."

Dealing with Contentment Busters

There are formidable forces that can challenge our most insistent efforts to realize contentment: an abiding sense of inner peace and well-being. Three of the mightiest contentment busters are *pressure of others*, *failure*, and *living with things we don't understand*.

Pressure from others can come in so many ways. Sometimes people, including family members, co-workers, bosses, and church members, expect too much from us. At other times, the pressure comes in the form of feeling misunderstood or under appreciated by others. And, there are those instances when we just seem to remain on someone's hit list no matter what we do. If we are to experience sustained inner peace and well-being, we have to find ways to defend our peace against the intended and unintended pressuring thoughts and behaviors of others. Two actions may prove helpful. First, we must disconnect our inner contentment from outer validation. That is to say: we must not allow our contentment to hinge on what others think or don't think about us. Plant your peace in who you are and who you are becoming, not in who others want you to be. Second, learn to be satisfied with your best, especially when others aren't. For some you'll never be or do enough. So, learn to let your best be enough.

Failure is another major contentment buster. Few things can bring us down so quickly as a sense of having missed the mark, of having irresponsibly let ourselves and those we love down. Perhaps the most effective medicine for the wound of failure is redefining failure. Most of us define failure in terms of misfortune and waste. Instead, dare to define failure as an unexpected learning opportunity. Anything you go through has the ability to teach you something new about life, and therefore enhance your living experience. What you consider to be failure may be reconfigured as an unexpected and unintended opportunity for unforeseen growth.

Finally, not understanding some occurrence or circumstance in life can undo our peace of mind and keep it undone for the long term. In addition to my Christian biblical faith that encourages trust in God through it all, including the darkest valley, I find the poet John Keats' theory of "negative capability" to be powerfully helpful. His theory, which is mentioned only once in his vast writings, suggests that persons are "capable of being in uncertainties, mysteries, doubts, without any irritable searching after fact and reason."

We can choose to live well with uncertainty. The poet, Rainer Maria Rilke, takes choosing to live positively with the awareness of the unresolved a step further by challenging us to "have patience with everything unresolved in your heart and try to love the questions themselves."

Being content with the unanswered involves our accepting the answer that we can't know it all right now. No doubt this is easier said than done. But, take heart, the land of not-knowing is not to be despised. Even more than in the land of knowing: all things are possible in the land of the unknown. The bruise of knowledge is limitation; the blessing of the unknown is limitlessness.

When doubts arise and hope is choked, know this: We never know enough to be completely hopeless. And, in the words of Howard Thurman: "The contradictions of life are not final."

Four Steps for Living Your Flame

In Scripture, the image for inspired labor is flame.

Moses is attracted to a new labor by a "burning bush."

Jeremiah embraces a call to speak God's word by feeling God's word as "burning fire" shut up in his bones.

The early church moves from fear to fearlessness in the wake of a great awakening characterized by "tongues of fire."

Our best offerings to the world are the things we are on fire about. When we are doing what we feel God's passion to do, God is glorified, we are fulfilled, and others are inspired. On the other hand, failing to perform our passion can cause recurring seemingly unexplainable sadness, and, believe it or not, deep fatigue. Even more heavy and wearying than the fatigue of overwork is the tiredness resulting from our not doing what we deeply want to do.

What do you deeply want to do? What are you on fire about? Here are four steps to help you begin to answer these questions:

1. Grab a pen or pencil and paper, find a quiet spot, and simply be still.

2. Ask yourself this question: "What work in the world would I do for free?" Reflect on your answers.

3. Begin to dream and devise a plan that will allow you to perform in the area of your passion as soon as possible.

What the Swan Said One Morning

Take time

each day

to feed your soul

with something

other than obligation.

—KBJ

Sacred Aspiration: Keeping Up with Growing Up

One of my favorite quotes comes from the late legendary pianist, composer, and bandleader, Duke Ellington. Creator of over 2,500 songs, when asked which was his favorite, he responded, "My next one." Ellington chose to live on and love the growing edges of his musical expression and development. For him, pushing his musical limits was one of the most exciting things about being alive.

In a world where it is often a challenge to just keep up, we must be intentional about our sacred opportunity to keep growing up.

Consider copying and posting the following five questions to help you keep up with the holy adventure of growing up:

1. What real risks have I taken lately?

2. How am I pushing my limits?

3. What am I exploring for the first time?

4. Where am I being challenged and stretched?

5. In what ways do I feel myself changing?

P.S. Fear of failure is one of the great obstructions to growing up. That being so, perhaps a declaration is in order: *Death without the possibility of revival to the fear of failure!*

The Difference between Contentment and Complacency

The best rest includes a feeling of contentment: a sense

of peaceful satisfaction about what we have already accomplished, including the lessons we've learned from our mistakes and so-called failures. Some persons resist allowing themselves to feel content for fear of becoming complacent. Remember this distinction: contentment receives new dreams and visions; complacency rejects new dreams and visions. Contentment replenishes our energy and enthusiasm for the challenging new adventures up ahead.

In order to press on with enhanced clarity and strength, we must pull back with deliberate intention and confidence. And, when you do, allow yourself to feel blessed in the deep places. Let yourself down easy in the soothing waters of God's grace. There are few things in life more dynamic than a rested body, and a rested soul.

7 Contentment Affirmations:

1.
"I float light and easy in the waters of contentment."

2.
"I am who I am; I have what I have; all is well."

3.
"I dare to let myself be satisfied."

4.
"As I say yes to grace, grace says yes to me."

5.
"It is well with my soul."

6.
"My cup is always running over."

7.
"Just being alive is a blessing."

Personal Reflection/Group Discussion Questions

What is contentment to you?

_____

_____

_____

_____

_____

How important are aspiration and achievement to you?

_____

_____

_____

_____

_____

How can we burn out in the pursuit of achievements?

_____

_____

_____

_____

_____

How can contentment be a friend to aspiration?

_____

_____

_____

_____

_____

Think of five ways to live a better balance of aspiration and contentment.

_____

_____

_____

_____

_____

Personal Journal Page

Affirmations:

_____

_____

_____

_____

_____

Questions:

_____

_____

_____

_____

Reflections:

_____

_____

_____

_____

_____

CHAPTER SEVEN
BELIEVE IN GOD
BEYOND "GOD"

"But I find that Your will knows no end in me, and when old words die out on the tongue, new melodies break forth from the heart; and where the old tracks are lost, new country is revealed with its wonders."
—Rabindranath Tagore

"The supreme happiness in life is the conviction that we are loved."
—Victor Hugo

"God's being with us does not hinge on our being with God."
—KBJ

Going after "God"

Any book by eminent professor Stephen Hawking is noteworthy. His acclaimed *A Brief History of Time* became an international publishing phenomenon, translated into 40 languages, and selling almost 10 million copies worldwide. His latest, *The Grand Design*, includes a grand assertion: The universe does not need "God" in order to explain its existence. Hawking suggests, "Spontaneous creation is the reason why there is something rather than nothing, why the universe exists, why we exist." Thus, in Hawking's view, the grand design need not have a "Grand Designer."

In fact, "God" has been denied in several recent bestselling books. Going after God is "hot." *God is not Great, The God Delusion, and Breaking the Spell* are just a few of the works that question unquestioned belief in "God," and the associated easy endorsement of religion. These works offer fresh, and in some cases, compelling presentations of traditional sociological and theological arguments against religious belief, including suspect historical texts which religious groups continue to abide by and receive as truth, unquestioned moral hypocrisy amongst religious adherents and leaders, institutional endorsement of hideous crimes of oppression, and the continuation of damning and harsh suffering in the world, especially among the young and the innocent.

In addition to such printed works, new movies challenge belief in "God" and religion. *"The God who Wasn't There"* touts itself as being a film "beyond belief." Noted television personality, Bill Maher, lends his sharp wit to a film that made its way into major theaters around the world. *"Religulous"* is an impressively researched and undeniably humorous critique of the dark shadows of religious zeal, including ignorance, self-righteousness, and, worst of all, violence. The film carries a passionate plea to denounce religion and as much as religion is about "God," a passionate plea to denounce "God," for the sake of our world's survival. Because of the threat of nuclear war, the film argues, we can ill afford more war, especially the worst kind of war, "holy war."

I hope you can tell from my brief explanation of these recent expressions of what some have referred to as "neo-atheism," that such expressions are not being made by people who are diseased in some way. (When I first heard persons speak about "atheists," their tone signaled a group of people who were sick in some way. The sentiment expressed by some of my Christian friends was that you had to be sick, if not evil, not to believe in God. Ironically, I would later learn that many so-called believers may not be atheists in theory, but they are atheists in practice. They don't say, "There is no God "; they just live like it.) People who challenge "God" don't do so because of disease, but because of dis-ease. And, their dis-ease is easy to understand given the hideous deeds done for the cause of religion, and in the name of "God."

My Discomfort with "God"

While reading some of the forementioned books and watching the movies, I had to face an undisputed fact, I, too, was at odds with religion and with "God." I remember remaining in my seat for many minutes after viewing *"Religulous."* The last one left, I still could not move from my seat. Dreadful questions entered my mind: *Could I have been so wrong all these years? Is religion and "God" more problems than solution in today's world? As clergy, am I a part of the problem?* These questions, and more like them, haunted and hunted me for days. And, then, it hit me, "God" was at fault, but not God.

"God" is our limited perception of GOD, that HOLY OTHER which cannot be fully named and comprehended. No matter what we think about God, our thoughts fall short, way short, of God. Our estimations, no matter how splendid and glorious or cutting and scathing, never say all there is to say about God. There is God beyond "God": a reality that transcends all our thoughts and deeds, the good, the bad, the ugly, and the beautiful. There is God beyond "God": a Reality, I believe, whose essence is unconditional love and who has never had nor ever will have anything to do with the lowest things done in the name of religion and in honor of "God," our incomplete notions of divinity usually constructed in our own image and designed for our own ends and preferences. The books and the movies are attempting to bring "God" or god down; no one comes close to bringing God, GOD, down.

The Saving Grace of God Beyond "God"

The story is told of a cleaning woman who worked at a large university. One evening while working, she came

upon a lecture hall in which the speaker was presenting on the topic: *The Death of God*. As the lecturer
proceeded, the woman grew more and more inter-
ested and disturbed. When he concluded his remarks,
the speaker welcomed comments and questions. A
few people responded, for the most part, affirming the
stance taken by the lecturer. Finally, the cleaning lady
raised her hand to be recognized. Acknowledged, she
spoke slowly, "Sir, did I understand you to say that God
was dead?" The lecturer responded politely, "Yes, you
did." The woman paused and then said, "I see. Well,
in that case I have a suggestion for you. The next time
you say that God is dead, you should add *as far as you
know*, because as far as I know, God woke me up this
morning. As far as I know, God clothed me in my right
mind. As far as I know, God started me on my way. So
then, the next time you say God is dead, say as far as
you know."

Distinguishing between God(GOD) who is beyond
comprehension and critique, and "God" who is our
incomplete perception of divinity, is not just some
theoretical device to protect God from atheistic attack. Believing in a God who always transcends our
thoughts and beliefs, who is always BIGGER, means
that we can confidently hold onto a positive belief in
GOD, no matter what is said about "God." We can
dare to believe that there is always a presence and
power in the world, waking us up, clothing us in our
right minds, and starting us on our way.

The Persistent Presence

In the aftermath of his astonishing resurrection, Jesus

made a promise to some followers gathered on a mountain. (See Matthew 28:16-18) He promised to "be with them always." The touching promise is all the more meaningful when you consider that according to the Scripture not all gathered on the mountain that evening were with Jesus, "some doubted." There were those in attendance who had serious reservations about the continued validity and viability of Jesus after his public, dreadful, and undeniable death. Yet, Jesus promises to be with them, all of them, always. That's right, Jesus doesn't just make the promise to those who are displaying high faith; low and no-faith folks are assured of his constant companionship, as well, whether they like it or not.

God is with us, whether we affirm God or not. God need not be acknowledged to be in attendance. God need not be avowed to be around. God's being with us does not hinge on our being with God. How amazing is that grace!

Daring to See God in New Ways

For over 20 years now, it has been my honor to teach at a school I graduated from 30 years ago, Andover Newton Theological School in Newton Centre, MA. In May, 2009, it was my blessing to offer the Baccalaureate prayer.

What I prayed reflects my growing faith in God beyond "God," God beyond my closed, familiar, and safe perceptions of God:

A Prayer for Theological School Graduates

I pray for and with these graduating,
yet still journeying
students of wonder and word.
May they be gifted with ministries that are
faithful and uncanny, and
holy and whimsical.
And, should their spirituality become
too isolated, lofty or stuffy,
let them remember
the lighthearted dance of the Nazarene,
whose liberating work
erupted at a wedding feast
and ended at a seaside fish fry.
Finally, for now, Marvelous Holy One,
Who loves us all madly,
please continuoulsy mess with their
"Master of Divinity" degrees
so that sometimes they will read
not "Master of Divinity," but rather
"Magic of Divinity"
Or
"Melody of Divinity"
Or
"Mystery of Divinity"
    Amen

Every "Good Morning" Has God in It

I enjoy walking, especially early in the morning. Once while walking in a park in Alexandria, Virginia, I had two very special experiences. In the first, I was walking along the narrow path curving a circle around a beautiful pond, when I came upon three women walking a couple of dogs. I stepped aside to allow them easier passage. As I moved back onto the path, the last person in the group, an elderly woman of Asian descent, smiled and said, "Good Morning" so gently and sweetly that it startled me, in a delightful sort of way. Her "Good Morning" was more than mere acknowledgment of my presence; it was genuine *appreciation* of my presence.

Upon finishing my walk, I sat at a picnic table to celebrate my morning devotional. An important part of my devotional is imagining receiving God's love. I do this in several ways, including seeing and feeling myself swimming in God's love, and kneeling beneath a waterfall of God's lavish acceptance. My intent is to awaken myself anew to the fact that I am the beloved of God, in such a way that I actually feel God's love in my very being. On this day, at the precise moment when I closed my eyes, bowed my head, and was about to imagine receiving God's love, I heard a bellowing but cheerful "Good Morning!" I looked up and saw a park sanitation worker looking downward, while picking up trash. I looked behind me to make sure that her greeting was meant for me. Seeing no one else around, I responded with a heartfelt, if delayed, "Good Morning."

Moments passed. As the park worker went about collecting

more litter, I realized that her greeting was still speaking to me. Her morning greeting to this stranger sitting in the park was so deliberate. It didn't matter that we didn't know each other; she held nothing back in heralding her morning blessing. Perhaps before I saw her bowed head, she saw mine, and perceiving that I may be feeling despondent about something, she wanted to give me reason to look up.

Two words, "Good Morning," offered up and out in meaningful and memorable ways. Wonder of wonders, though especially true of these two, every "Good Morning" has God in it—and come to think of it, every "good afternoon," "good evening," and "good night."

Always

Always,

God looks upon us

With eyes

Wild with compassion

And possibility.

Always.

—KBJ

Holy Lunacy

Early one morning,

in the stillness

of being

held and loved

by God,

in my peripheral vision,

I saw

an angel

doing a cartwheel.

—KBJ

A Question

God to you:

May I have

this dance?

—KBJ

Come On and Take a Grace Ride!

Living in Grace is

letting yourself ride gleefully

atop God's shoulders.

—KBJ

7 Faith in God Beyond "God" Affirmations:

1.
My soul is continually nurtured by God's love and grace.

2.
"I am not afraid to dance with God."

3.
"I am a dancing spirit who delights in whirling and and twirling with God."

4.
"I relax free and easy in the soft and soothing grace of God."

5.
"Because God is well, I am well."

6.
"God's grace is more than enough."

7.
"God's being with me does not hinge on my being with God."

Personal Reflection/Group Discussion Questions

How did you view God when you were younger?

_____

_____

_____

_____

_____

How has your vision of God changed through the years?

_____

_____

_____

_____

_____

How does your vision of God influence your life?

_____

_____

_____

_____

Describe your prayer life.

_____

_____

_____

_____

_____

How important is having an understanding of God being within you?

_____

_____

_____

_____

Personal Journal Page

Affirmations:

_____

_____

_____

_____

_____

Questions:

_____

_____

_____

_____

_____

Reflections:

_____

_____

_____

_____

_____

CHANGE OF ADDRESS NOTICE

MOVED TO GRACE

WHERE I NOW RESIDE

IN GREAT JOY AND PEACE!

THE SEVEN GRACE SOLUTIONS

1.
Learn to Rest

2.
Live From Acceptance, Not For Acceptance

3.
Loosen Strings to Needs and Expectations

4.
Live at a Sacred Pace

5.
Claim Your Inner Calm

6.
Balance Aspiration with Contentment

7.
Believe in God Beyond "God"

<u>A Parting Blessing</u>

Be encouraged.

Don't let detours deter your commitment,

and deadends deaden your enthusiasm.

Fight on; move on; press on.

There are clearer skies just over the hill.

—KBJ

PLEASE PASS THE GRACE!

If *Say Yes to Grace* has been a special blessing to you, and I hope it has, please pass on its life-enhancing message through one or more of the following ways:

1. Tell family members, friends, and co-workers about the book via word of mouth or social networking sites like Facebook and Twitter.

2. Announce the book in your church/club/organization newsletter.

3. Include a brief book excerpt in a church, school, business, or other institutional newsletter. Please add the following at the end of the excerpt: Copyright © 2010 by Kirk Byron Jones, www.sayyestograce.com

4. Join the *Say Yes to Grace* Facebook fan page and encourage others to do so.

5. Write a brief review of the book at amazon.com, barnesandnoble.com, or another online book website.

6. Give gift copies of the book to family members, friends, and co-workers.

7. Encourage an individual or organization to provide a financial grant for copies to be given to students at high schools and universities around the world. Please email me at kjones58@aol.com for additional information.

Thank you so much for passing the grace.

ALSO BY KIRK BYRON JONES

Rest in the Storm: Self-Care Strategies for Clergy and Other Caregivers

Addicted to Hurry: Spiritual Strategies for Slowing Down

The Jazz of Preaching: How to Preach with Great Freedom and Joy

Morning B.R.E.W.: A Divine Power Drink for Your Soul

The Morning B.R.E.W. Journal

Holy Play: The Joyful Adventure of Unleashing Your Divine Purpose

For more free inspirational articles, and E-Book and Audio resources, visit

www.kirkbjones.com

Visit with Dr. Jones on his Facebook pages

"Kirk Byron Jones" and "Say Yes to Grace"

and on Twitter at "KirkByronJones"

THE SOUL REFRESHING CONTINUES!

GRACE GRAPES

365 Small Meditations to Sweeten Your Soul

Kirk Byron Jones

Coming Spring, 2011

"Amazing Grace, How Sweet the Taste"

ABOUT THE AUTHOR

Reverend Kirk Byron Jones is a graduate of Loyola University and Andover Newton Theological School, and holds a Doctor of Ministry degree from Emory University and a Doctor of Philosophy degree from Drew University.

A pastor for over 20 years, Dr. Jones was the founding minister of Beacon Light Baptist Church in New Orleans, and Senior Minister at Calvary Baptist Church, Chester, PA; Ebenezer Baptist Church, Boston, MA; and the First Baptist Churches of Randolph and Whitman, MA. He is currently pastor of First Baptist Church, Tewksbury, MA. Throughout his pastoral ministry, Rev. Jones has served on various religious and civic committees at the local and national level.

An adjunct professor of ethics and preaching at Andover Newton Theological School and Boston University

School of Theology, Dr. Jones serves as guest preacher and teacher at churches, schools and conferences throughout the United States. His writings have been published in various journals, including The Christian Century, Leadership, and Gospel Today, Pulpit Digest, and The African American Pulpit, a quarterly preaching journal he co-founded in 1997.

Dr. Jones is the author of several best-selling books including:

Rest in the Storm: Self-Care Strategies for Clergy and Other Caregivers

Addicted to Hurry: Spiritual Strategies for Slowing Down

The Jazz of Preaching: How to Preach with Great Freedom and Joy

Morning B.R.E.W.: A Divine Power Drink for Your Soul

The Morning B.R.E.W. Journal

Holy Play: The Joyful Adventure of Unleashing Your Divine Purpose

Rest in the Storm, was one of just 40 books and films selected by Sojourners Magazine as "The Best Resources for Social Change." The compilation contains the works of historic and contemporary luminaries, including Sojourner Truth, Henri Nouwen, Stephen Spielberg, and Martin Luther King, Jr.

CPSIA information can be obtained at www.ICGtesting.com
Printed in the USA
LVOW061910160911

246645LV00001B/2/P